A NATION IMAGINED

First West Indies Test Team

Lord Constantine greets H.R.H. King George V, July 10, 1928.

Hilary McD Beckles

Foreword by Wes Hall

First published in 2003 by
Ian Randle Publishers
11 Cunningham Avenue
Box 686
Kingston 6
Jamaica
www.ianrandlepublishers.com
and
Centre for Cricket Research,
the University of the West Indies,
Cave Hill Campus,
Barbados

© Hilary McD Beckles

All rights reserved – no part of this publication may be reproduced, stored in a retrieval system, or transmitted in any form, or by any means electronic, photocopying, recording or otherwise without the prior permission of the author or publisher.

ISBN 976-637-161-X paperback
ISBN 976-637-162-8 hardback

A catalogue record of this book is available from the National Library of Jamaica

Cover photos: Learie Constantine, *Cricket in the Sun,* (Stanley Paul & Co. Ltd.)
Cover design: Vaneisa Baksh, with Anya de Souza and Jeffrey Pataysingh of Lonsdale Saatchi & Saatchi Advertising Agency Limited
Book design: Vaneisa Baksh
Production: Lonsdale Saatchi & Saatchi Advertising Agency Limited
Electronic Prepress: Impact Prepress Limited
Printing: Zenith Printing Services Limited

Contents

Dedication
Acknowledgements
Foreword

Introduction

A NATION IMAGINED

1. WAR AND PEACE	1
2. AN AMERICAN BEGINNING	4
3. THE ROAD TO ENGLAND	7
Multiracialism	9
First Tour to England	11
White Batsmen, Black Bowlers	19
The Fight for Test Status	20
4. CAMPAIGN FOR TEST STATUS	22
George Challenor	24
5. THE 1928 TEST TOUR	31
Second Class Still	33
6. WINNING BATTLES IN A LOSING WAR	40
First Test	40
The First Four-Pronged Pace Attack	45
Second Test	54
Third Test	58
7. REFLECTIONS ON A JOURNEY	60
The Exclusion of George Headley	61
Appendix	
The West Indies Cricket Guide, 1928	64

Contents

THE 1928 ARCHIVES

Arrival of West Indian Team	i
Tour Directory: West Indies in England, 1928	ii
Derbyshire v West Indies at Derby, 5-8 May 1928	iii
Essex v West Indies at Leyton, 9-11 May 1928	v
Surrey v West Indies at Kennington Oval, 12-15 May 1928	vii
Oxford University v West Indies at Oxford, 16-18 May 1928	ix
Marylebone Cricket Club v West Indies at Lord's, 19-22 May 1928	xi
Cambridge University v West Indies at Cambridge, 26-28 May 1928	xii
Ireland v West Indies at Dublin, 4-6 Jun 1928	xiv
Middlesex v West Indies at Lord's, 9-12 Jun 1928	xvi
Yorkshire v West Indies at Sheffield, 13-15 Jun 1928	xix
Minor Counties v West Indies at Exeter, 16-19 Jun 1928	xx
1st TEST: England v West Indies at Lord's, 23-26 Jun 1928	xxii
Northamptonshire v West Indies at Northampton, 27-28 Jun 1928	xxvii
Lancashire v West Indies at Manchester, 30 Jun-3 Jul 1928	xxix
Yorkshire v West Indies at Leeds, 4-6 Jul 1928	xxxi
Nottinghamshire v West Indies at Nottingham, 7-10 Jul 1928	xxxiii
Warwickshire v West Indies at Birmingham, 14-17 Jul 1928	xxxv
Worcestershire v West Indies at Worcester, 18-19 Jul 1928	xxxvii
2nd TEST: England v West Indies at Manchester, 21-24 Jul 1928	xxxviii
Wales v West Indies at Llandudno Cricket Club Ground, 25-27 Jul 1928	xliv
Leicestershire v West Indies at Leicester, 28-31 Jul 1928	xlvi
Somerset v West Indies at Bath, 1-3 Aug 1928	xlviii
Glamorgan v West Indies at Swansea, 4-7 Aug 1928	l
Gloucestershire v West Indies at Bristol, 8-10 Aug 1928	lii
3rd TEST: England v West Indies at Kennington Oval, 11-14 Aug 1928	liv
Sussex v West Indies at Brighton, 18-21 Aug 1928	lix
Hampshire v West Indies at Southampton, 22-24 Aug 1928	lxi
Kent v West Indies at Canterbury, 25-28 Aug 1928	lxiii
Harlequins v West Indies at Eastbourne, 29-31 Aug 1928	lxv
England XI v West Indies at Folkestone, 1-4 Sep 1928	lxvii
HDG Leveson-Gower's XI v West Indies at Scarborough, 8-11 Sep 1928	lxix

Dedication

For the pioneers on the first West Indies Test team:

Claude Vibert Wight

Clifford A. Roach

Cyril Rutherford Browne

Edward Lawson Bartlett

Edward Lisle Goldsworthy Hoad

Ernest A. Rae

Frank Reginald Martin

George Challenor

George Nathaniel Francis

Herman C. Griffith

James M. Neblett

Joseph A. Small

Learie N. Constantine

Maurice Pacheco Fernandes

O.C. "Tommy" Scott

Robert Karl Nunes

Wilton H. St. Hill

Acknowledgements

This book would not have been possible without the support and assistance of several people. The author wishes to thank the President of the West Indies Cricket Board, Rev. Wes Hall, for recognising the importance of the historic occasion and for thus committing the WICB to urging the book's publication in time for the 75th anniversary of West Indies Test status.

Alison Saunders-Franklyn, who handles the public relations aspects of the WICB, spent a great deal of energy organising and channelling resources to ensure that the project was incorporated into the wider celebration of the occasion.

Ahmed Reid spent many hours going through newspaper archives in London, to provide the rich, first-hand accounts of the 1928 season in England.

Sandra Newton competently transformed my hand-written drafts into legible typescript, and Ayanna Bowrin converted the occasionally hazy newspaper accounts into easily-read copy.

Anya de Souza and Jeffrey Pataysingh worked with Vaneisa Baksh to come up with the slightly unorthodox design of the book, which places the material from the 1928 archives to run parallel to the narrative, rather than at the end.

The staff at the Educational Media Services department of the Learning Resource Centre at the Cave Hill Campus was able to technically reproduce some of the fading images of 1928 which we were able to unearth, and to make them into clear pictures of the period.

Shell Antilles and Guianas Ltd. generously assisted in the book's production.

For these invaluable contributions, and those from everyone who assisted in one way or the other, my gratitude goes out wholeheartedly.

Foreword

Being president of the West Indies Cricket Board (WICB) is a great honour itself but to be placed in the circumstance of being responsible for giving appropriate effect to the 75th anniversary of West Indies Test status is special for countless reasons.

To reflect on the achievements of West Indian cricketers before gaining Test status in 1928, and beyond, requires an enlargement of the mind because of the incredible success in a relatively short time. The contribution of the Test pioneers remains fresh with many of the living veterans. As a fast bowler who wished to respect and celebrate the tradition of high speed from which I emerged, I am particularly aware of the foundation built by Lord Constantine, George Francis, and Herman Griffith on that inaugural tour. I grew up in Barbados under the great legacies of George Challenor, the opening batsman, and George Francis, the opening bowler, of the inaugural Test match at Lord's June 23-26. I knew Constantine and worked as a young man to enhance his legacy during my term as a Sports Commissioner in Trinidad and Tobago.

While we celebrate the first step onto a Test field, I am aware of the considerable amount of work our players must do to reclaim the Test pinnacle we occupied between 1978 and 1995. Through all of this, we have achieved many records, including the two uppermost in the public mind – Brian Lara's 375 Test innings and Courtney Walsh's 519 Test wickets.

In between the inaugural Test and recent achievements, we produced the great George Headley, nicknamed 'Atlas' because he carried our young team on his shoulders during the 1930s; the legendary 3Ws (Worrell, Weekes and Walcott); great opening pairs, Allan Rae and Jeff Stollmeyer, and Gordon Greenidge and Desmond Haynes; the incomparable allrounder Garfield Sobers; spinners of world class, Sonny Ramadhin, Alf Valentine and Lance Gibbs; a battalion of extraordinary fast bowlers, Charlie Griffith, Roy Gilchrist, Andy Roberts, Keith Boyce, Michael Holding, Malcolm Marshall, Joel Garner, Ian Bishop, Colin Croft, Courtney Walsh, Curtly Ambrose; middle order batsmen who set high, new global standards – Rohan Kanhai, Viv Richards, Clive Lloyd, Lawrence Rowe, Richie Richardson, Alvin Kallicharran, and other great ones, including wicket keeping sensations like Gerry Alexander, Jackie Hendricks, David and Deryck Murray, and Jeffrey Dujon. There was hardly a decade since 1928 in which a West Indies batsman was not considered the best in the world, and the consensus around Headley, the 3Ws, Sobers, Richards, and Lara has allies beyond the shores of the Caribbean. The same could also be said about the bowling department, as was the case

Foreword

with Lance Gibbs, and in recent times with Roberts, Holding, Marshall, Ambrose and Walsh.

These are great achievements by any standard, and when we reflect that Lloyd's team of the 1980s is considered the best Test team of all times, we have reasons to believe that the decision to grant us Test status in 1928 was an appropriate one, the inaugural performance notwithstanding.

Today we are in the planning stages of hosting the World Cup in 2007, and doing so within the context of global opinion that the West Indies brand of cricket remains exciting and creative, despite recent results.

It is a great pleasure and honour, then, to be associated with this commemorative book by Prof. Hilary Beckles that details the circumstances surrounding our journey to Test status in 1928, and an assessment of the tour. Over the years, he has made important analyses of West Indies cricket history, and I welcome this book as a timely contribution by the Director of the Centre for Cricket Research at our sister institution, the University of the West Indies.

The WICB has made a significant sponsorship investment in this text because we consider the 1928 inauguration a moment of such magnitude that it demands meaningful celebration. I hope it will be widely read and used as a site of reference for those with a literary interest in West Indies cricket, as well as the players, administrators, spectators and students, and, indeed, all those stakeholders of West Indies cricket who have brought us thus far and who will be with us in the years ahead.

Wes Hall
President
West Indies Cricket Board

Introduction

1928 was home to the first truly grand, all-inclusive West Indian celebration. A people with no previous opportunity to express a common imagination, West Indians found fulfilment in celebrating the historic event. Socially divided by a turbulent past, they rose in triumph with a single voice. Achieving Test status for West Indian cricketers in 1928, then, gave shape and form to a new phase in the political imagination of a fractured community. Finally, West Indians had built a monument to tower over their legacy of divided identity.

The team selected to engage the English in the inaugural Test series was understood in the West Indian world as the prime symbol of a nation imagined. They were emissaries of a national consciousness slow in the making, and long deprived of form by persistent colonialism that still gave no sign of a final retreat. The seminal political events of the next decade, featuring West Indians rising in popular opposition to second-class status within the empire, were ideologically informed by the spectacular success of cricketers.

The emerging national society summoned its cricketers to represent it in an international arena distinguished for nearly a century by its considerable prestige and symbolic cultural power. The West Indians had arrived at gates already entered by Australia and South Africa, though not as yet by India. Compared with its predecessors, the West Indian team was as different as the nature of imperial relations. The team of 1928 was not sent to England to play friendly 'cousin' cricket, but to represent a mentality that was determined to break free of the colonial scaffold. It was also put in the field to set out in clear parameters the infrastructure of something unprecedented in modern history – a multiracial nation built upon the principle of social equality and the unencumbered rule of merit.

As clearly imagined as the nation was in 1928, the team as an early symbolic representation indicated that considerable social work was still required to meet public expectation. Its leadership still resided in the hands of a traditionally privileged group whose performance on the field fell far short of the rule of merit. The startling exclusion of players from the Indian community concentrated in Guiana and Trinidad spoke as loudly as the inclusion of players from the scattered African community. The nation was only partially imagined, then, but there was intense social and political pressure focused on full attainment.

The use of a quota system in the team selection process

Introduction

was already an established part of the West Indian method. It secured pride of place for the major sugar-producing societies: Guiana, Trinidad, Jamaica and Barbados. There was no doubt that the cricket fraternity was a social product of the 'sugar boys'. This gave Barbados, the place with the purest pedigree in the plantation business, the greatest influence. The Leeward and Windward Islands, where the planter-merchant elite did not emerge from the emancipation process as an empowered political class, were kept at the periphery and treated like newcomers. Representatives of the 'big four' met in Barbados and settled matters relating to the journey to England.

Learie Constantine of Trinidad was the young rising star of the new dispensation, as was George Challenor of Barbados, the elder icon of the old days. Between these two pillars, a mixture of old and new ways embarked on the 'enterprise of the Indies'. On board were the dreams of a nation in the making. It was a difficult challenge, as social forces from the past and future combined to create tensions that determined outcomes on the field as much as they did beyond the boundary. On-the-field performance expectation invoked Constantine, George Francis and Herman Griffith. They occupied the bowling department of the team, a role assigned to the African community. Robert Karl Nunes, the aloof captain, who saw social distance from those under his command as an important instrument of governance, held power and authority.

A house separated is no home. The West Indies team, burdened with the cultural legacies of the region, but driven by the search for excellence, fell before the walls of an imperial structure determined to protect all within. Lacking cohesion and searching for an alternative strategy, the team found no inner links to withstand the clash of consciousness. Defeated with ease at the outset of the Test journey, the reflective team returned home to reconsider its relationship to public expectation. The "whitewash" experience stayed with Constantine as an open wound that held his game in focus as an element in the struggle for the nation imagined. He commented less than a decade later, at the height of his career, that he still dreamed of a day when the West Indies team would be selected entirely on merit and led by one who commanded equal respect on and off the field.

This narrative of the journey to Test status picks up the evi-

Introduction

dence at the close of the 18th century and ends with a compilation of match reports and statistics on the historic Test series. It is by no means an exhaustive empirical examination, but an account that sets out seminal cricket moments and underlying social processes along the way. It is a part of the discourse that puts in clear focus the making of the contemporary Caribbean as one of the greatest projects of modernity.

As a magical moment in West Indies cricket history the 1928 tour certainly deserves a major socio-cultural analysis. There is a wealth of empirical data to support such a study, and hopefully this text will serve to stimulate interest and spark concern for the future of intellectual discourse in West Indies cricket writing, so successfully championed by the late C.L.R. James and Michael Manley.

The timing of the publication speaks for itself. This year is the 75th anniversary of the 1928 West Indies inaugural Test tour. It falls in the midst of Sri Lanka's tour to the West Indies, a circumstance that should prompt reflection on the West Indies journey, as the already distinguished tourists are today relatively new to the Test arena.

As a text, its creation resides in years of conversation with Vaneisa Baksh, editor of the docu-text section that brings to life exciting sections of the 1928 tour archives. These discussions served to focus the work of the University of the West Indies' Centre for Cricket Research, established in 1994 at the Cave Hill Campus in Barbados as a research and publishing network. It is the fifth publication of the CCR, the third with Ian Randle Publishers, and the second as a collaborative effort with Baksh, who is principally responsible for its conceptual design, textual layout and production. The President of the West Indies Cricket Board, Rev. Wes Hall, endorsed the project and urged its publication to meet the celebratory purposes of June 2003, the 75th anniversary of the West Indies' first Test match.

In this spirit, it is presented as a gift to the West Indies cricket community, especially the pioneers of 1928, and, hopefully, will serve to remind future bearers of the torch of the magnificent West Indian journey to excellence.

Hilary Beckles
June 2003

1.

War and Peace

It all began in the heat of war. By the closing of the eighteenth century, the West Indian world had become a veritable field of war as French and English captains of armies contested for colonial turf. Thousands of English soldiers, garrisoned mostly in Barbados, but also in the Leeward and Windward Islands, entertained themselves with bats and leather balls while taking respite from hurling cannon balls at the French. The records of these early encounters between 1798 and 1838 reveal that keenly fought matches had become the favourites of civilian society. In this regard, the famous match played at St. Ann's Cricket Club, on the Garrison field outside of Bridgetown, between the Garrison XI and the 78th Regiment on May 12, 1838, may then be considered a useful marker of the 100-year long journey that culminated in West Indies Test status in 1928.

Distinguished cricket historians, such as the late C.L.R. James, Brian Stoddart, Frank Birbalsingh and Keith Sandiford, have contended that the English imperial cricket culture arrived laden with coded social messages conducive to empire building.

For this reason, the success of cricket in the West Indies during the nineteenth century was remarkably swift. It first penetrated the cultural world of the propertied white creole élite who embraced it as a celebration of the unbroken bond between themselves and their metropolitan 'cousins'.

The colonial élite moved swiftly to canonise organised cricket within its own definition of advanced culture. The earliest pioneers of the game intimated that it was part of the cultural tradition of the English gentry – and that the corresponding colonial class inherited what was logically

THE 1928 ARCHIVES

ARRIVAL OF
WEST INDIAN TEAM

Sixteen members of the West Indian team who, under the captaincy of R.K. Nunes, are to tour this country this summer, arrived at Avonmouth yesterday in the Camito. The weather when they disembarked, and when they reached Paddington, was dismal in the extreme, there being a bitterly cold, driving rain. They were met in London by Mr. R.H. Mallett, representing the M.C.C., and Major the Hon. L.H. Tennyson.

The party consisted of R.K. Nunes, E.L. Bartlett, C.R. Browne, G. Challenor, L.N. Constantine, jun., E.L.G. Hoad, F.R. Martin, C. Roach, W. St. Hill, J.A. Small, C.V. Wight (the vice-captain), M.P. Fernandes, O.C. Scott, G. Francis, H.C. Griffith, and J. Neblett, with Mr. J.E. Scheult, the assistant manager. E.A. Rae is travelling *via* New York.

R.K. Nunes said that he had high hopes of his side, all of whom felt delighted that they had been accorded Test Match rank. He said that he regarded the team as an extremely well-balanced one in every respect, being even stronger than that of 1923, the batting being stronger, and there being a greater variety of bowling and much better fielding.

He pointed out that the team includes three fast bowlers, and while Francis is as accurate and fast as he was in 1923, Constantine, so brilliant at cover-point, when here before, had shown wonderful improvement and was now faster than either Francis or Griffith. He said that he considered that the visits of English sides encouraged the game in the West Indies, but he thought that the last team, under the captaincy of Major Tennyson, began playing too soon after their arrival to do themselves full justice. His attention had been drawn to the proposal to be placed by the Lancashire County Club before the Advisory County Cricket Committee concerning the control of tours in which Test Matches are played, Nunes said that the West Indies make no actual guarantee in connexion with tours, but there is an implied guarantee for the reason that cricket in the West Indies is governed by the West Indies Board of Control, which includes two delegates from each colony. If a loss occurs then it is borne by the colonies.

Nunes, Browne, Challenor, Constantine, Fernandes, Small, and Francis took part in the last tour in this country.

–The Times,
Tuesday, April 17, 1928, Page 7

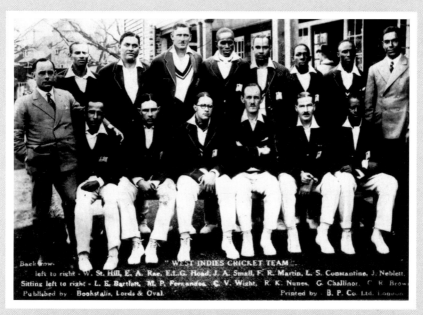

A postcard depicting the 1928 West Indian touring team to England.

theirs by right of ancestry. It was only a matter of time, however, before the civil rights struggles promoted cricket as a popular trans-racial cultural expression. The desire of coloured, black, Indian and Chinese communities to play cricket their own way seemed to have developed in direct proportion to the white élite's determination to exclude them. It is debatable whether these marginalised groups 'loved' it simply because the white élite did, or whether, in the absence of other mass activities, it was able to capture their creative imagination and prove useful in their cultural and political struggles.

The Rev. Grenville John Chester, whose literary sketches on the black poor of Barbados in the aftermath of slavery are frequently cited by social historians, tells us in 1869:

"The labouring classes in Barbados are badly off for amusement. Tops and marbles seem almost the only sports of the school children, but when encouraged they take kindly to cricket. But it is hard to find places to play in, and parochial cricket clubs are either above or below the notice of the local clergy. Thus dancing is almost the only amusement, and the people dance well and gracefully."

West Indies cricket, by the end of the nineteenth century, had been transformed from a minority élite 'English' sport into the region's first expression of popular mass culture. It had broken out of the mould represented by garrisoned

Children playing cricket in Antigua in the 1880s.

Tour Directory

West Indies in England, 1928

1. - Derbyshire v West Indies at Derby, 5-8 May 1928
2. - Essex v West Indies at Leyton, 9-11 May 1928
3. - Surrey v West Indies at Kennington Oval, 12-15 May 1928
4. - Oxford University v West Indies at Oxford, 16-18 May 1928
5. - Marylebone Cricket Club v West Indies at Lord's, 19-22 May 1928
6. - Cambridge University v West Indies at Cambridge, 26-28 May 1928
7. - Ireland v West Indies at Dublin, 4-6 Jun 1928
8. - Middlesex v West Indies at Lord's, 9-12 Jun 1928
9. - Yorkshire v West Indies at Sheffield, 13-15 Jun 1928
10. - Minor Counties v West Indies at Exeter, 16-19 Jun 1928
11. - **1st TEST:** England v West Indies at Lord's, 23-26 Jun 1928
12. - Northamptonshire v West Indies at Northampton, 27-28 Jun 1928
13. - Lancashire v West Indies at Manchester, 30 Jun-3 Jul 1928
14. - Yorkshire v West Indies at Leeds, 4-6 Jul 1928
15. - Nottinghamshire v West Indies at Nottingham, 7-10 Jul 1928
16. - Warwickshire v West Indies at Birmingham, 14-17 Jul 1928
17. - Worcestershire v West Indies at Worcester, 18-19 Jul 1928
18. - **2nd TEST:** England v West Indies at Manchester, 21-24 Jul 1928
19. - Wales v West Indies, Llandudno Cricket Club Ground, 25-27 Jul 1928
20. - Leicestershire v West Indies at Leicester, 28-31 Jul 1928
21. - Somerset v West Indies at Bath, 1-3 Aug 1928
22. - Glamorgan v West Indies at Swansea, 4-7 Aug 1928
23. - Gloucestershire v West Indies at Bristol, 8-10 Aug 1928
24. - **3rd TEST:** England v West Indies, Kennington Oval, 11-14 Aug 1928
25. - Sussex v West Indies at Brighton, 18-21 Aug 1928
26. - Hampshire v West Indies at Southampton, 22-24 Aug 1928
27. - Kent v West Indies at Canterbury, 25-28 Aug 1928
28. - Harlequins v West Indies at Eastbourne, 29-31 Aug 1928
29. - England XI v West Indies at Folkestone, 1-4 Sep 1928
30. - HDG Leveson-Gower's XI v West Indies, Scarborough, 8-11 Sep 1928

A NATION IMAGINED

Kensington Oval in Barbados during the tour of an English XI in 1902.

English military men, and had spread into the plantations, and the villages and towns. In so doing, cricket traversed a wide geographical space and slowly embraced all social classes and races. "Every self-respecting colony," noted Algernon Aspinall at the end of the nineteenth century, "has one or more cricket clubs, and the keenest interest is taken in the game especially during the winter months in alternate years, when an Inter-colonial Cricket Cup is competed for by representative teams from Barbados, British Guiana and Trinidad". Cricket became the leading leisure institution of a colonial élite in search of a modern method of social differentiation. Seized by blacks, Indians and coloureds, however, it became the focus around which an intensive civil rights war was waged for social and cultural equality and justice.

THE 1928 ARCHIVES

Derbyshire v West Indies
County Ground, Derby - 5, 7, 8 May, 1928 (3-day match)

Result: West Indies won by 2 wickets
Umpires: RD Burrows and TW Oates

Derbyshire 1st innings
H Storer	c Nunes	b Francis	36
D Smith		b Francis	17
GM Lee	c Constantine	b Browne	19
*GR Jackson	c Constantine	b Browne	1
AG Slater	c Small	b Francis	12
JM Hutchinson		b Small	26
TS Worthington	lbw	b Small	6
AW Richardson	c Fernandes	b Small	1
LF Townsend	not out		12
+H Elliott	c Nunes	b Browne	4
W Shardlow	c Challenor	b Browne	2
Extras	(b 13, lb 9, nb 1)		23
Total	**(all out, 72.1 overs)**		**159**

Francis 20-6-48-3 Small 14-8-15-3 Constantine 16-5-29-0
Browne 22.1-6-44-4

West Indies 1st innings
G Challenor	c Elliott	b Townsend	75
CA Roach	c Storer	b Slater	16
MP Fernandes	c Elliott	b Townsend	14
FR Martin	c Elliott	b Slater	8
WH St Hill	c Jackson	b Slater	8
JA Small	c Smith	b Slater	7
CR Browne	c Shardlow	b Slater	11
CV Wight	not out		7
*+RK Nunes	c Elliott	b Slater	1
LN Constantine	lbw	b Slater	0
GN Francis		b Slater	0
Extras	(b 5, lb 2, w 1)		8
Total	**(all out, 83.3 overs)**		**155**

Shardlow 8-2-20-0 Storer 3-0-6-0 Worthington 18-1-39-0
Lee 13-4-18-0 Slater 16.3-8-24-8 Townsend 25-12-40-2

Derbyshire 2nd innings
H Storer	c Small	b Francis	9
D Smith		b Small	26
GM Lee	c Browne	b Francis	11
*GR Jackson	c&b	Constantine	63
AG Slater		b Browne	12
JM Hutchinson	c Martin	b Browne	3
TS Worthington		b Browne	7
AW Richardson	c Constantine	b Browne	17
LF Townsend	c St Hill	b Constantine	3
+H Elliott	c Nunes	b Francis	13
W Shardlow	not out		0
Extras	(b 8, lb 4, nb 1)		13
Total	**(all out, 67.4 overs)**		**177**

Francis 20-3-57-3 Small 9-3-18-1 Constantine 18-3-45-2
Browne 18.4-6-37-4 Martin 2-1-7-0

West Indies 2nd innings (target: 182 runs)
G Challenor	lbw	b Lee	22
CA Roach		b Townsend	28
MP Fernandes		b Townsend	8
FR Martin	c Elliott	b Lee	18
WH St Hill		b Slater	12
JA Small		b Townsend	19
CR Browne		b Lee	4
CV Wight	run out		12
*+RK Nunes	not out		21
LN Constantine	not out		31
Extras	(b 3, lb 3, w 1, nb 3)		10
Total	**(8 wickets, 104.3 overs)**		**185**

DNB: GN Francis.
Lee 29-14-43-3 Slater 23.3-14-27-1 Townsend 30-12-58-3
Shardlow 8-216-0 Worthington 14-5-31-0

2.

An American Beginning

In 1886 the first West Indian team was selected for the explicit purpose of playing outside of the region. An all-white team went on a tour of Canada and the United States where the cricket culture could claim a longer pedigree than in the West Indies. As early as 1844, Canada and the United States had clashed in their first 'international' – 24 years before the much acclaimed Australian Aboriginal tour to England in 1868. English teams toured Canada and the United States in the summer of 1859, by which time Canadians had declared cricket their official sport. English teams also toured the United States in 1868 and in 1872. On the latter occasion, none other than the legendary Dr. W.G. Grace participated, scoring an expected and impressive 142 against a Toronto side. Australia toured Canada for the first time in 1878, so that when the West Indies team arrived eight years later, the Canadian public was long accustomed to international cricket. In all, 13 matches were played. The West Indies team won six, lost five and two were drawn. On the whole, it was a fairly mixed sort of tour from the point of view of results.

In short, the West Indies cricket team, on its first overseas tour, was humiliated and made to feel quite inferior to various American cricket clubs. The performance in Canada was satisfactory, but the United States proved a formidable challenge.

A summary of the tour by Captain George Wyatt, a middle order batsman from Demerara, Guiana, however, painted a less grim picture. Noting that for many the proposed tour was perceived at home "as rather a farce", he made reference to the pioneering nature of the project.

Despite being "sneered and laughed at by many more

WEST INDIAN TEAM AT DERBY

CHALLENOR IN FORM

The West Indies began their first-class programme at Derby on Saturday. They dismissed a strong Derbyshire eleven on a good wicket in three hours and a half for only 159 runs, and followed this up with such sound batting that, putting together a total of 107 runs for the loss of one wicket, they finished the day only 52 runs behind with nine wickets standing. This advantage was obtained by splendid all-round cricket. The bowling, which was varied in pace, was accurate and the fielding reached a high standard. Added to this, Challenor treated a company of 4,000 people to a superb display of batting in the evening.

At the start the Derbyshire batsmen showed there was little wrong with the pitch, for Storer and Smith played excellent cricket for an hour in an opening partnership that yielded 52 runs. Smith is a left-handed batsman and a right-hand bowler. He made a number of well-timed off-side strokes before a good-length ball knocked down his leg stump. Storer hit four 4's – splendid strokes to leg and clean drives – in obtaining his 36 out of 57, but later only Hutchinson offered serious resistance to the bowling. Small, a right-handed medium-paced bowler, met with marked success, his three wickets being secured at the small cost of five runs each. Browne, who is similar in pace, took four for 44, and Francis, the fast bowler, had an analysis of three for 48.

George Challenor

Left with roughly two hours' batting, the West Indies' opening pair, Challenor and Roach, showed no disposition to hurry. Still, in a few minutes under the hour they had 50 runs on the board. Three runs later Roach, a right-handed defensive batsman, was taken at second slip. Then Challenor and Fernandes proceeded to obtain a complete mastery over the bowling. Challenor completed a faultless 50 out of 70 in 80 minutes, and so far he has hit nine 4's in his 70 not out.

–*The Times,*
Monday, May 7, 1928, Page 7

WEST INDIES WIN AT DERBY

AN INTERESTING FINISH

Whatever may be in store for them in the future, the West Indies team in the opening first-class match of their tour have proved themselves to be a resourceful side. The whole side batted with marked steadiness at Derby yesterday, and had the satisfaction of beating Derbyshire, who last season finished fifth in the County Championship, by two wickets.

From the beginning of this match there has been a dogged fight for supremacy, and though the scoring generally has been low the match produced bowling and fielding well above the average. Quite an interesting position had been reached when the final day's play was begun yesterday, for with all their wickets in hand in their second innings, the West Indies required 163 runs in order to win.

From the start Challenor and Roach played very carefully, the first 50 runs occupying an hour and 20 minutes. Challenor left after the first-wicket stand had produced 55 runs, and then Derbyshire met with such success that the tourists at the luncheon interval had four men out for 86.

The position certainly warranted the care that was subsequently exercised by Martin and Small, and, though they took as long as an hour to put on 29 runs for the fifth wicket, it had the effect of wearing down the home attack. However, when Lee in one over got rid of Martin and Bourne for the addition of eight runs, the West Indies apparently had lost their advantage. Indeed, the position became desperate when Wight, in his anxiety to obtain runs, had his wicket thrown down with the total at 149. Meanwhile Nunes had batted with great determination and scored 11 runs in two overs.

The turning point came when he was joined by Constantine at the fall of the eighth wicket. Constantine took a bold course, and in ten minutes' vigorous batting he hit five 4's and a 3, supplementing this with an 8 off Worthington in the next over. Nunes went on playing well at this critical period, and shortly after 4 o'clock the West Indies captain, with a splendid stroke to the boundary off Slater, made the winning hit.

–*The Times,*
Wednesday, May 9, 1928, Page 7

Kensington Oval in Barbados, 1948.

than most people imagine", the team was able to experience an overseas tour, and this helped to build confidence among the cricket fraternity. It was not the strongest West Indies team, noted Captain Wyatt, though it might very well have been the wealthiest. The players were expected to personally fund their own trip, and this financial arrangement excluded a fair number of more talented players. The entire cost of the tour amounted to "near £1,000", an average of £71 or $340 per man for nine weeks.

The West Indians had followed the English into North America, and had not done as well, but were looking forward to an exciting future. Captain Wyatt, who averaged 9.13 on tour, made comments that signalled the developmental vision held by this touring party for West Indies cricket:

"The ball has been set a-rolling now, and if the result of our recent tour gives us many visits in the West Indies from our Canadian and American friends, and wakes up our Island neighbours and our own Colony to move about amongst each other and further afield, in the interest of the noble game, something tangible and well worth having will have been gained, and the writer fully and well recompensed for what trouble he has taken in the matter.

"But a hint to our island neighbours must be given. Some proper and really strong move must be made to secure permanent and good cricket grounds everywhere in the West Indies where the game is to take any standing, and let us hope that nowhere will this latter not be the case. In Barbados especially, the rendezvous and headquarters for all passenger steamers, there ought certainly to be the best ground in the West Indies, and we trust that the 'blot' (for such it is) of not having such a ground will not continue much longer."

THE 1928 ARCHIVES

Essex v West Indies
County Ground, Leyton - 9, 10, 11 May, 1928 (3-day match)

Result: Match drawn
Umpires: LC Braund and F Parris

Essex 1st innings
LC Eastman	c Constantine	b Francis	11
JA Cutmore	lbw	b Francis	24
J O'Connor	c Nunes	b Constantine	29
CAG Russell	c Small	b Martin	147
MS Nichols		b Small	6
*JWHT Douglas		b Small	53
C Bray		b Francis	31
AB Hipkin	c Fernandes	b Roach	30
EC Thompson	not out		19
+FE Hugonin	c Fernandes	b Constantine	0
RN Shorter		b Francis	1
Extras	(b 13, lb 5)		18
Total	**(all out, 124.4 overs)**		**369**

Francis 26.4-5-73-4   Browne 18-4-42-0   Constantine 31-7-96-2
Small 32-2-81-2   Hoad 2-0-22-0   Martin 6-1-17-1
Roach 9-2-20-1

West Indies 1st innings
G Challenor	c Hipkin	b O'Connor	62
CA Roach	c Douglas	b Nichols	45
MP Fernandes	c Shorter	b O'Connor	16
ELG Hoad	c Hugonin	b Nichols	11
FR Martin	lbw	b O'Connor	53
JA Small	c Hugonin	b Nichols	12
CV Wight	c Russell	b Eastman	7
LN Constantine		b Nichols	130
CR Browne		b Shorter	10
*+RK Nunes	c Hugonin	b O'Connor	11
GN Francis	not out		2
Extras	(b 8, lb 6, w 4)		18
Total	**(all out, 121.2 overs)**		**377**

Nichols 36-7-117-4   Eastman 25-4-66-1   Shorter 17-6-41-1
O'Connor 38.2-6-120-4   Hipkin 5-1-15-0

Essex 2nd innings
JA Cutmore	c Constantine	b Hoad	77
EC Thompson		b Martin	21
J O'Connor	c Nunes	b Martin	93
LC Eastman	not out		58
Extras	(b 1, lb 9)		10
Total	**(3 wickets, 75.3 overs)**		**259**

DNB: CAG Russell, MS Nichols, *JWHT Douglas, C Bray, AB Hipkin, +FE Hugonin, RN Shorter.

Francis 6-1-13-0   Small 24-5-75-0   Constantine 5-0-24-0
Hoad 7-1-31-1   Martin 22.3-5-51-2 Roach 11-1-55-0

AN INTERESTING GAME AT LEYTON.

The West Indies match against Essex, at Leyton, yesterday, finished in an even position, as, in reply to the Essex total of 369, the West Indies lost six wickets for 245 runs. G. Challenor and C. Roach put on 100 runs for the West Indies first wicket, and it is probable that during the early weeks of the tour they will have to depend on Challenor to give them a good start to an extent that would be embarrassing were it not for the fact that Challenor looks so

—The Times, Friday May 11, 1928 Page 7

MATCH NO. 2

West Indies in England, 1928

The first West Indies XI to play against an English XI in Barbados in 1902.
Standing from left: (The Umpire), F. Hinds, J. Burton, Shepherd.
Seated (middle row): P.I. Cox, A.E. Harragin, H.B.G. Austin, C.H. King,
G.C. Learmond. Front row: J. Woods, O.H. Layne and V. Challenor.

The following year the Americans returned the visit, but played against territorial sides rather than a West Indies team. It was a weak team and was defeated by Trinidad, Demerara, Jamaica and Barbados. The Barbados and Jamaica matches were billed as 'America vs Barbados' and 'Gentlemen of America vs All-Jamaica' respectively, but the evidence was now clear that the Civil War had ravaged American cricket culture leaving it a poor third to baseball and football.

THE WEST INDIES AT LEYTON

MANY CATCHES DROPPED

Essex, in their match against the West Indies at Leyton yesterday, made 358 runs for seven wickets, a score which should at any rate make them safe from defeat. From the West Indies point of view the day was tragic in that some really good and intelligent bowling was broken, not against the rock of the batsmen's defence, but against the even more heart-breaking rock of their own fielders' mistakes.

Excuses, of course, could be found for them, as the weather was cruelly cold, especially in contrast to the halcyon days of a week ago, and one or two of the catches were not the kind one likes to come across early in May – but it is not excuses the West Indies want.

Their catching was definitely bad, just as their ground-fielding was good, but while they saved many runs they lost others, partly by an occasional faulty placing of the field – Francis, for instance, should have had a long-leg before the runs scored off him in that direction made one imperative – and partly, although this is admittedly a small matter, by a certain forgetfulness in backing up.

In scoring 124 for the loss of four wickets before luncheon Essex did more than they should have done, for the West Indies missed three or four catches which, on a warmer day, would have been easy. The two West Indies fast bowlers, G. Francis and L.N. Constantine, made the ball come off the pitch at sufficient pace to make that great defensive player, J.W.H.T. Douglas, play at short, rising balls and be thankful he missed them. After Eastman had been caught in the slips by Constantine off Francis, O'Connor came in to play an innings which, although it might have been cut shorter by M.A. Fernandes, one would nevertheless have liked to have seen prolonged.

Constantine was inclined to bowl short, and three times O'Connor hooked balls off his forehead round to the boundary, but in attempting the stroke a fourth time he got under the ball and gave a high, spinning catch to the wicket-keeper. C.R. Browne who, swinging and breaking across the wicket from off to leg, had three fieldsmen on the leg-side, bowled very well, and once Russell, getting a well pitched-up ball on the end of his bat, dropped it provokingly between them, but although Nunes brought back his fast bowlers, Russell and Douglas remained together till luncheon, when their scores were 36 and nine respectively.

–The Times,
Thursday, May 10, 1928, Page 7

L. N. CONSTANTINE SCORES A CENTURY

The match between Essex and the West Indies ended at Leyton yesterday in a draw, the West Indies having the satisfaction of leading their opponents on the first innings by eight runs.

Except for one brief period there was a refreshing tendency right through the innings to make a definite stroke at every ball, and one can well imagine the West Indies confounding the captain who dare declare and set them runs to get in the last innings before the clock has made the making of them a human impossibility. Their catching, on the other hand, was not reassuring.

For the fact that they succeeded in passing the Essex total the West Indies have a truly great innings by L.N. Constantine to thank. C.R. Browne and R.K. Nunes both played valuable parts in keeping up their wickets, but it was Constantine who captured the imagination and who got the runs. He was attacking the bowling all the time, and, although as is almost inevitable when a batsman is not being over particular about the balls he picks out to hit, a certain number of them went in any direction except the one he intended, yet it was impossible not to see, even through the mis-hits, that Constantine was no mere village-green "slogger," but a batsman with strokes that should put some of our modern batsmen to shame.

Constantine, indeed, belongs to a time when batting was on a more generous scale than it is to-day. In his sweeps to leg, not pulls or hooks, but strokes made with a full swing of the bat and a balance got by dropping on to the right knee, he showed his affinity to those cricketers who have become legendary names, and in his back-play – one ball he played from R.N. Shorter, drawn back on his stumps, rattled up against the sight-screen – he showed a firmness and strength of wrist that reminded one of that great batsman, K.L. Hutchings.

–The Times,
Saturday, May 12, 1928, Page 6

3.

The Road to England

West Indians were now looking towards England as the direction to go in the consolidation of their cricket and the thrust to place themselves on an international stage. England, of course, was recognised as the premier cricketing nation on account of its claim as the 'inventor' of the organised game. It was also undeniably a case of white West Indian colonials seeking approval and recognition of their achievements from their 'motherland' in this cultural arena. By the early 1890s, they seemed frantic (similar to the Australians two decades earlier) in the quest for approval from the Marylebone Cricket Club (MCC). They desperately wanted a contest with England, but the English were slow to respond.

Both Wyatt and L.K. Fyfe of Jamaica, the captain and vice-captain respectively of the first 'West Indies' team, had sought separately to arrange West Indies tours of England in 1888 and 1889. Their efforts were not successful, and it seemed then that the region's first encounter with England would take place under the circumstance of a touring English team playing against individual colonies. This occasion finally came when Slade Lucas assembled an English eleven which arrived in the region in January 1895.

Implicit within the thinking behind this first encounter was some measure of English contempt for West Indian cricketing abilities. The touring team was made up of low-level amateurs with one, maybe two, recognised players – hardly a first-class eleven. Yet, thousands of West Indians came out to greet them with great fanfare wherever they went. The common English perception of West Indian standards was confirmed by the tour results. The English teams won 10 of the 16 matches and lost only four. In front of a crowd in excess of 6,000 at Kensington Oval, Bridgetown, the Barbados team

THE 1928 ARCHIVES

Surrey v West Indies

Kennington Oval, London - 12, 14, 15 May, 1928, (3-day match)

Result: Match drawn
Umpires: HR Butt and J Hardstaff

Surrey 1st innings

JB Hobbs	c Constantine	b Francis	13
A Sandham		b Constantine	26
HT Barling	c Constantine	b Griffith	1
TF Shepherd	c Fernandes	b Griffith	4
DR Jardine	c Neblett	b Francis	58
*PGH Fender	c Small	b Constantine	45
CE Daily	c Fernandes	b Constantine	0
RJ Gregory		b Constantine	96
HA Peach		b Francis	24
ACT Geary		b Francis	4
+EWJ Brooks	not out		3
Extras	(b 11)		11
Total	**(all out, 78.4 overs)**		**285**

Francis 20.4-3-77-4 Griffith 15-4-40-2 Constantine 22-5-81-4
Small 14-2-43-0 Neblett 5-0-21-0 Martin 2-0-12-0

West Indies 1st innings

G Challenor	c Gregory	b Shepherd	37
CA Roach	c Shepherd	b Gregory	46
+MP Fernandes	c Fender	b Shepherd	23
WH St Hill	c Fender	b Shepherd	18
FR Martin	c Fender	b Shepherd	19
JA Small	c Fender	b Gregory	33
LN Constantine	c Geary	b Peach	50
JM Neblett		b Peach	9
*RK Nunes	lbw	b Shepherd	42
HC Griffith	not out		4
GN Francis		b Fender	1
Extras	(b 22, b 14)		36
Total	**(all out, 118.4 overs)**		**318**

Geary 19-6-34-0 Peach 26-6-63-2 Gregory 23-6-49-2
Fender 17.4-6-33-1 Shepherd 33-9-103-5

Surrey 2nd innings

JB Hobbs	not out		123
A Sandham	not out		108
Extras	(b 18, lb 3, nb 1)		22
Total	**(0 wickets declared, 70 overs)**		**253**

DNB: HT Barling, TF Shepherd, DR Jardine, *PGH Fender, CE Daily, RJ Gregory, HA Peach, ACT Geary, +EWJ Brooks.

Francis 17 3-48-0 Griffith 15-1-55-0 Constantine 11-1-35-0
Small 16-2-54-0 Neblett 8-0-33-0 Martin 3-1- 6-0

West Indies 2nd innings (target: 221 runs)

G Challenor	c Fender	b Peach	5
CA Roach		b Peach	1
+MP Fernandes		b Peach	2
WH St Hill		b Peach	5
FR Martin	lbw	b Gregory	10
JA Small		b Peach	25
LN Constantine	not out		60
JM Neblett	not out		4
Extras	(b 6)		6
Total	**(6 wickets, 40 overs)**		**118**

DNB: *RK Nunes, HC Griffith, GN Francis.

Geary 7-3-12-0 Peach 13-3-25-5 Gregory 7-2-25-1
Fender 7-0-41-0 Shepherd- 6-3- 9-0

MATCH NO. 3

West Indies in England, 1928

was beaten. St. Vincent, not yet considered a cricketing colony, however, succeeded in defeating the Englishmen.

Reports in the West Indies press indicate that colonials, in spite of receiving a sound thrashing by the English team, were overcome with excitement by the experience. Press references suggest that colonial sport writers expressed in no uncertain terms the sense of low self-esteem seemingly evident among West Indians with respect to the English. In their losing game, Barbados scored 517 in the second innings, a West Indies record at the time, and an achievement that presented an opportunity for the local press to unilaterally claim colonial 'arrival', and to indicate in a self-denying way its reverence for the standards supposedly established by their opponents. In Bridgetown, *The Times* of February 9, 1895, reported:

"Englishmen at home and abroad must have learnt with mixed feelings the news wired on Tuesday evening announcing to the world pre-eminent achievements that Barbados batted the whole day and had, at the call of time on Tuesday evening, still 3 wickets to fall with the score standing at the magnificent total of 359. Three centuries and a half would have been as fine a cricketing feat for a Colonial team that could possibly be accomplished in the presence of English batsmen and bowlers of renown, that would cause any Colonial combination to be inordinately proud of. But when it comes to be thought of that a team of cricketers in this little England beyond the seas could put in the field capable of greater things, though having for their opponents stalwarts hailing from the home of cricket, it seems to us to suggest a something not dreamt of in our cricketing philosophy. A West Indian batting record has been established in the cricket annals of these parts, and whatever the pride and elation we feel in knowing that it has been given to Barbadians to chronicle that fact in their history, cannot but be pardonable. That Barbados possessed the ability to compile 517 runs in a single innings was what the most judicious observers of our boys' play or even the most sanguine spirits among us would have described as belonging more to the region of exuberant imagination than to be within the bounds of possibilities."

As soon as the Lucas team departed, West Indians rejoiced to hear that arrangements were being made in England for other touring teams to test the 'colonial cricket steel'. In 1896, two English teams – one led by A. Priestly (later Sir) and the other by Lord Hawke – arrived in the West Indies. Popular opinion was that both teams were stronger than the Lucas XI, though all were still considered amateurs.

The family linkages of empire being what they were,

THE 1928 ARCHIVES

WEST INDIES AT THE OVAL
MISSED CATCHES

Surrey scored 285 runs in their first innings against the West Indies at the Oval on Saturday.

A score of 285, even if the wicket is perfect, is respectable enough, and anyone who was not on the ground might well imagine that Surrey had batted easily and comfortably for their runs. Nothing could be further from the truth. Had the West Indies slip-fielders been comparable in excellence to their fast bowlers, Surrey might easily have been out for 175; had their slips been packed with Braunds and A.O. Joneses, they might have been out for a total which, considering the strength of their batting and the easiness of the wicket, would have been sensational. The fact is that the West Indies can do what no county side in England can do, and that is to keep a fast bowler on at one end from the start of a long innings to the finish; but the fast bowler is dependent on his slips, and, if his slips fail him, then, sooner or later, the heart goes out of him.

Twice on Saturday, first when P.G.H. Fender and then when Gregory went in, the West Indies looked likely to go through Surrey and leave D.R. Jardine with an eloquent 40 or so not out, but on both occasions the chance was thrown away; in the first instance through a certain faulty placing of the slips, and a lack of that indefinable sense, the hall-mark of a great slip-fielder, that can anticipate the stroke before it is played, and in the second through a definitely missed catch.

–The Times, Monday, May 14, 1928, Page 5

DINNER TO WEST INDIES TEAM

The West Indies team were the guests at dinner of the Surrey County Cricket Club at the Oval on Saturday. The Surrey president, Mr. J.H. Longman, had on his right and left the West Indies captain and vice-captain, R.K. Nunes and C.V. Wight, respectively. Others present, apart from the players of the two teams, included Lord Lucan (president of the M.C.C.) Sir R.W. Rutherford, Major the Hon. L.H. Tennyson, Mr. R. Slade Lucas, Mr. R. Aucher Warner, Mr. W.E. Roller, Mr. M.R. Jardine, Mr. H. Hughes Onslow, Mr. R.H. Mallett, Mr. A.H.H. Gilligan, Mr. W.A. Gilligan, and Mr. W. Findlay, the vice-chairmen being Mr. H.D.G. Leveson-Gower, Mr. A.M. Latham, Mr. M. Howell, and Mr. R.C.N. Palairet.

–The Times, Monday, May 14, 1928, Page 5

WEST INDIES AVERT DEFEAT
LONG INNINGS BY HOBBS AND SANDHAM

The match between Surrey and the West Indies at the Oval ended yesterday in a draw, the West Indies at the close of play needing 103 runs to win with four wickets in hand.

Up till 12 o'clock or so yesterday morning the only alternative to a draw seemed a victory for the West Indies, but, after Hobbs and Sandham had scored 253 together without being separated, Peach, at one time taking four wickets for six runs, made a sensational victory for Surrey possible, but J.A. Small and L.N. Constantine averted a danger that had never been foreseen. The quick fall of wickets enabled Constantine to play his third successive innings of 50 or over. The West Indies have less reason to be depressed by the 253 – Hobbs and Sandham, content to play well within themselves on a perfect Oval wicket, are capable of going on for ever – than by the fact that, once the sting is taken out of their fast bowlers, there is so little left. Small, it is true, can keep down runs, but, at any rate until the rain comes, their left handed bowlers do not look like causing batsmen the slightest trouble.

When Hobbs and Sandham went on with their innings yesterday morning it became immediately obvious that neither of them intended to risk a repetition of the 1923 defeat and give the West Indies slips a chance of brightening a reputation that Saturday had left sadly tarnished.

For the first half-hour or so there was a very faint chance that the unexpected might happen, and both Constantine and G.N. Francis bowled as though that hope was strengthening their arms. Hobbs had a maiden over from Constantine in that he twice missed balls at which he played confidently, and once he found another, which was meant to trickle to short leg, shoot off to the slips. In spite of the gently admonitory pats this occasioned, it was clear that the pitch was, if anything, even less inclined to help the bowlers than it had been on the two previous days.

–The Times, Wednesday, May 16, 1928, Page 7

Priestly's team contained Dr Gilbert Elliot, a Barbadian, who refused to play in the Barbados match on the grounds that he could not compete against his own country. The Hawke team also included a West Indian: Pelham Warner, the distinguished Trinidadian. Both teams did well against colonial sides. Jamaica and Demerara received humiliating defeats, while Trinidad won two matches against each side. The Barbadian team won 2-1 in three games against the Priestly side, and lost one of the two games against the Hawke side.

The impressive record of the Trinidad team, which had hitherto been considered the weakest of the 'Big Four', drew particular attention for one special reason. Pelham Warner, star batsman of Hawke's side, who scored a hundred against the Barbados team, studied the matter and concluded that Trinidad's victories were due to the inclusion of two black professional bowlers, J. Woods and C.P. Cumberbatch. This was a new and critical development in West Indies cricket, and signalled the beginning of the non-racial process of democracy in selection policy.

J. Woods and C.P. Cumberbatch, two of Trinidad's best bowlers.

Multiracialism

Black professionals had long been excluded in 'all-island' teams for 'friendly' games. Without its black players, it was recognised, the Trinidadian team was no match for Barbados and Demerara. Warner considered this development of great importance to West Indies cricket. He concluded that only the integration of blacks into colonial and West Indies teams could raise the standard, increase competitiveness, and liberate the regional cricket culture for the quantum leap into world recognition.

It was the racist mentality in Barbados and Demerara especially, Warner argued, that continued the suffocating all-white race policy. Furthermore, he said, the talent of black players was necessary to "make the game more popular

THE 1928 ARCHIVES

Oxford University v West Indies
The University Parks, Oxford - 16, 17, 18 May, 1928 (3-day match)

Result: Match drawn
Umpires: GW Ayres and A Stoner

West Indies 1st innings

FR Martin	c Crawley	b McIntosh	17
CA Roach	c Skene	b McIntosh	45
WH St Hill		b McIntosh	4
CV Wight	c Benson	b Tew	2
JA Small		b Skene	15
EL Bartlett		b Hill-Wood	85
LN Constantine	c Pataudi	b Hill-Wood	36
EA Rae	c Garland-Wells	b Skene	0
*+RK Nunes	not out		76
OC Scott	c Crawley	b Skene	18
HC Griffith	c Crawley	b Tew	22
Extras	(b 2, lb 2)		4
Total	**(all out, 96.5 overs)**		**324**

McIntosh 25-4-78-3 Hill-Wood 22-2-60-2 Tew 14.5-2-80-2
Skene 27-8-62-3 Garland-Wells 8-1-40-0

Oxford University 1st innings

*AM Crawley	c Constantine	b Scott	55
Nawab of Pataudi		b Griffith	2
PGT Kingsley		b Griffith	0
PVF Cazalet	c Scott	b Constantine	11
NM Ford	c Rae	b Small	68
HM Garland-Wells	c Wight	b Constantine	55
+ET Benson		b Griffith	5
CKH Hill-Wood	c Scott	b Constantine	10
RW Skene	c Griffith	b Small	27
AM Tew		b Griffith	15
RIF McIntosh	not out		4
Extras	(b 4, lb 7, nb 1)		12
Total	**(all out, 90.4 overs)**		**264**

Griffith 24-5-74-4 Small 17.4-7-26-2 Constantine 23-7-71-3
Scott 13-1-67-1 Martin 13-7-14-0

West Indies 2nd innings

FR Martin	c Benson	b McIntosh	15
CA Roach	c Pataudi	b McIntosh	16
WH St Hill	c Garland-Wells	b Hill-Wood	58
EA Rae	c Benson	b Hill-Wood	10
JA Small	not out		106
EL Bartlett	c Kingsley	b Tew	21
LN Constantine		b Crawley	69
CV Wight	not out		8
Extras	(b 7, lb 3)		10
Total	**(6 wickets, 71 overs)**		**313**

McIntosh 14-4-35-2 Hill-Wood 14-1-52-2 Tew 14-2-74-1
Skene 12-3-39-0 Kingsley 6-0-49-0 Crawley 6-0-28-1
Garland-Wells 5-0-26-0

MATCH NO. 4 — West Indies in England, 1928

WEST INDIES' GOOD SCORE.

CLEAN HITTING AGAINST OXFORD.

At the close of play in the Parks yesterday the West Indies, in their match with Oxford University, who are still without M. A. McCanlis, were all out for 324 runs. Three or four dropped catches apart, the Oxford out-cricket was satisfactory. E. T. Benson was always doing a little more than can

—The Times, Thursday, May 17, 1928, Page 7

locally", and could assist in assuring "great and universal enthusiasm amongst all classes of the people". The first West Indian team selected for a proposed tour to England, he insisted, should include "four or five" black players, since this would be the only way to prevent embarrassments against county teams.

The late 1890s, then, witnessed calls for the introduction of blacks into inter-colonial cup competitions and West Indies touring teams. With a voice as influential as that of Pelham Warner's, the West Indian cricket élite felt compelled to rethink selection policies. There had been no opposition in England to the presence of blacks in competitive cricket. By this time, such crude expressions of racial separation were confined to the colonials, who found it particularly difficult to consider blacks as equals in any sphere of social activity. During the 1890s, Barbados had stated its refusal to play against Trinidad in the Challenge Cup if they included black players. In the 1897 competition, Trinidad arrived in Barbados without its black bowling stars and was massively beaten by an innings and 235 runs.

If Trinidad had not learnt its lesson by this time, white Barbadians had received the message when, in 1899, Spartan, the coloured middle-class team, won the island's Challenge Cup, defeating traditional whites-only teams. It undermined their ideology of white supremacy in cricket culture.

The rise to dominance of Spartan within Barbados cricket clearly indicated that racism in West Indies cricket was a major constraint and an embarrassment to the highest ideals of cricket culture. The Trinidadians had initiated the policy of selection on merit, and at the end of the century, the word was out that nutrients for the future growth of West Indies cricket could be found in large quantities within the black communities.

This raised a number of significant questions about the social organisation of West Indies cricket. Would whites accept blacks and Indians as equals within the boundary, and in the social activities beyond it? Were facilities available to all races to acquire the 'personality' that was required of colonial representation? Would the whites allow other races access to leadership in this vital area of West Indian life? These issues generated controversy throughout the region, while the English cricket world listened with a mixture of amusement and horror.

Responding to the debate over the relative quality of

THE 1928 ARCHIVES

OXFORD'S REPLY

A GREAT CATCH BY L. N. CONSTANTINE

Play was only possible for 3 hours in the match between Oxford University and the West Indies in the Parks yesterday, but in that time Oxford did quite well to score 202 runs for six wickets in reply to the West Indies' total of 324.

N.M. Ford made 68 and A.M. Crawley, not for the first time this season, played a splendid innings, an innings that was cut short by a catch by L.N. Constantine that nobody who saw it will forget for a long time. R.K. Nunes was not well yesterday, and C.V. Wight captained the side in his place.

The weather was dull and cold when Crawley and the Nawab of Pataudi opened the Oxford innings to the bowling of Constantine and H.C. Griffith. With the total at 15 Pataudi played far too late at a ball from Griffith that looked almost a yorker, and had his leg stump knocked out, while the next ball bowled P.G.T. Kingsley, who went back to it in a half-hearted way. P.V. Cazalet, who can play fast bowling, looked like getting runs, but at 32 he was completely deceived by Constantine's slow ball, played too soon, and was easily caught at mid-off.

Crawley and N.M. Ford then proceeded to add 55 runs together. It would be difficult to over-praise Crawley's innings. His bat moves with a beautiful freedom and correctness, and he made runs all round the wicket. If anyone on the ground doubted Crawley to be a really first-class batsman, two strokes he made off O.C. Scott in one over must have convinced him – the first, a cut that had enough "wrist" behind it to leave a deep third-man standing, and the second, a magnificent drive, that raced away between cover-point and extra-cover-point. He reached his 50 by forcing a length ball of J.A. Small's round off his body, a stroke he made more than once, but in the next over he was caught. Scott was bowling round the wicket, and Crawley, with his feet beautifully placed for the stroke, got hold of a ball on the leg-stump. It looked a 6 all the way from the bat, and would have been had not Constantine on the boundary at square-leg leapt into the air, stretched out his right hand, and brought off a catch that looked impossible. H.M. Garland-Wells, who immediately scored 10 runs on the leg-side off Scott, stayed in with Ford until luncheon, when the score was 114 for four wickets.

–The Times,
Friday, May 18, 1928, Page 7

WEST INDIES DRAW AT OXFORD

CENTURY BY J. A. SMALL

The match between Oxford University and the West Indies, which after Oxford's recovery from a bad start never looked as though it could have a definite finish, ended in a draw at Oxford yesterday, the West Indies leading by 60 runs on the first innings.

In spite of the fact that the batting is rather over-dependent on A.M. Crawley, one of the best batsmen the Universities have turned out since the War, Oxford have the making of a good side. The experimenting that has been going on is all to the good, and it has shown that there will not be room at Lord's for all those capable of making 50 against first-class bowling. If there is room for improvement in the fielding, there are signs that the improvement will come about, and the side has the great advantage of possessing a wicket keeper who, coming fresh into first-class cricket, can give one the impression he has been playing it all his life, and playing it exceedingly well. What the side really needs at the moment is the return of M.A. McCanlis. The bowling, although steady, does not look capable of "going through" a side, but McCanlis may make all the difference.

Oxford increased their score from 202 for six wickets to 264 yesterday morning. C.K. Hill-Wood, who may make a good many runs this season, got well over the fast bowlers to start with, but one ball did not quite come off the bat as he wished, and V.C. Scott made a good catch low down at fourth slip. A.M. Tew made some good, and some distinctly curious, runs before he had his leg-stump knocked out of the ground in attempting a more than usually rustic stroke, but R.W. Skene stayed to play thoroughly sound cricket until he played forward to Small, got the ball on the edge of his bat, and gave H.C. Griffith at point a catch that went to him shoulder high. Oxford were lucky in that they found the West Indies inclined to drop catches.

–The Times,
Saturday, May 19, 1928, Page 6

black and white cricketers in Barbados, a leader writer for *The Reporter* argued that "there is absolutely no provision of playgrounds attached to primary and elementary schools" attended by black children, and yet their fidelity to the methods and the values of the game was well inculcated. Blacks, it was widely understood, had established their own cricket culture about the 'gullies' of plantation villages and streets of urban ghettos. Their game was learnt at the community level, rather than in a formal way, within the school system. For them, cricket had become as instinctively cultural as religion.

Behind Spartan's success in Barbados in 1899, was a well of black talent waiting to be tapped. Professional black teams, such as the Fenwicks and Carrington cricket clubs, both working class organisations, represented this pillar within Barbados cricket. Just as it was known that these teams had defeated established Challenge Cup sides, but were excluded from any formal competition on the basis that they were professionals, so it was also known that racial prejudice was the principal reason.

By the end of the century, blacks, coloureds, Indians, Chinese and other ethnic minorities were poised to force their way *en masse* into first-class colonial cricket, and therefore to secure eligibility for West Indies teams. Everything was in place for it. When it was announced in 1899 that Lord Hawke had invited a West Indian team to tour England in the summer of 1900, the time for the grand 'English' debut of multiracial West Indies cricket had arrived.

First Tour to England

P.F. Warner's brother, R.S. Warner, was appointed captain of the West Indies team. A selection committee, representing all the West Indian cricket territories, met in Trinidad in January 1900 with the mandate to choose a representative team. Shortly thereafter the news came: five blacks were selected to the touring party of 15. These players were Fitz Hinds (Barbados), W.J. Burton (Demerara), C.A. Ollivierre (St. Vincent), and J. Woods and L.S. Constantine (Trinidad). Pelham Warner wrote:

"It has been decided to include black men in the coming team, and there is little doubt that a fairly strong side can be got together. Without

Marylebone Cricket Club v West Indies
Lord's, London - 19, 21, 22 May 1928 (3-day match)

Result: Match drawn (Rain stopped play)
Umpires: HR Butt and TW Oates

Marylebone Cricket Club 1st innings
FSG Calthorpe	not out		21
JW Hearne	c Challenor	b Browne	29
DR Jardine	not out		10
Extras	(b 3, lb 1, w 1)		5
Total	**(1 wicket, 31 overs)**		**65**

DNB: JC White, HJ Enthoven, JC Clay, APF Chapman, +RT Stanyforth, TO Jameson, EH Hendren, FJ Durston.

Francis 5-1-9-0 Griffith 1-0-3-0 Constantine 4-2-3-0
Browne 11-3-19-1 Small 5-1-19-0 Martin 5-1-7-0

A RAIN-SPOILED DAY
WEST INDIES MEET M.C.C.

One of the most interesting matches which were begun on Saturday was that between the M.C.C. and the West Indies at Lord's. The West Indies lost the toss, and, of course, the M.C.C. went in. The Hon. F.S.G. Calthorpe, having fulfilled the first duty of a captain in winning the toss, went in first himself.

The wicket was soft and gave the bowlers no help. At the same time, one must say that L.N. Constantine bowled one ball which entirely flabbergasted J.W. Hearne. The ball broke back a good eight inches, beat the bat, beat the batsman, and missed the tops of the stumps. After that Hearne played some brilliant cricket. He had both the fast bowlers, Constantine and Francis, under control. Of course, it was not their wicket, but against ordinary batsmen they might have been most unpleasant.

Calthorpe, usually a good hitter, played very slow cricket for a batsman of his ability. Hearne played extraordinarily well, and nobody wanted to bowl to him. His hooking is that of the first-class player, and the bowler does not like being treated in the way that Hearne does treat him. Hearne was well caught at short-leg by Challenor off a good hit.

Browne seems to be an exceptionally clever bowler. He is a leg-break bowler who occasionally bowls the ball which goes straight on. He is of the type of Braund, but must not be confused with the googly bowlers.

After Hearne had been dismissed D.R. Jardine came in. The interest in this batsman is considerable, because he has been suggested to play for England in Australia. Jardine played Browne quite easily, and, considering how well Browne was bowling, that was a great test of cricket. He saw Small very quickly, and played him very confidently and very well.

In the last ten minutes before luncheon one would have liked to have seen Constantine and Francis on again. The fast bowlers, no doubt, would have been put on immediately after the luncheon interval, but the rain came on, and no further play was possible.

–The Times,
Monday, May 21, 1928,
Page 7

these black men it would have been quite absurd to attempt to play first-class counties, and no possible benefit would have been derived from playing those of the second class only. The fielding will certainly be of a high class. The black men will, I fear, suffer from the weather if the summer turns out cold and damp, as their strength lies in the fact that their muscles are extremely loose, owing to the warm weather to which they are accustomed. Woods takes only two steps and bowls as fast as Mold! Englishmen will be very much struck with the throwing powers of these black men, nearly all of them being able to throw well over a hundred yards. On the whole, I feel pretty confident that the team will attract favourable attention all round, and my view is, I know, shared by many sound judges of the game. The visit of any new team to England is always an experiment, attended with more or less possibilities of failure; but that they will be a failure I do not for a moment think, and in any case West Indian cricket will be greatly improved."

The tour was not given first-class status as there seemed to have been considerable belief among English officials that the West Indians were not ready for 'serious' competitive cricket. *Wisden* described the tour as an "experiment", but P.F. Warner had no doubt that by its end the West Indians would be ready for the first-class designation.

The English press warmly welcomed the "second-class" West Indians but criticised their apparent "slipshod and lazy" attitudes. The *Boy's Own Paper (BOP)*, however, was particularly concerned to inform its readers about the "great nov-

One of the cartoons appearing in the press, depicting the West Indians as unable to handle 'cultured' food, even as they devour it greedily.

THE 1928 ARCHIVES

Cambridge University v West Indies
F.P. Fenner's Ground, Cambridge - 26, 27, 28 May, 1928 (3-day match)

Result: West Indies won by 9 wickets
Umpires: LC Braund and HR Butt

Cambridge University 1st innings

*FJ Seabrook	lbw	b Francis	0
TC Longfield		b Francis	3
KS Duleepsinhji		b Small	41
MJL Turnbull	c Nunes	b Constantine	27
RWV Robins	c Neblett	b Browne	30
BH Valentine		b Browne	10
WG Morgan	not out		22
MJC Allom		b Constantine	1
LG Irvine		b Constantine	0
+T Martin		b Constantine	1
ED Blundell		b Constantine	0
Extras	(b 3, lb 3)		6
Total	**(all out, 47.3 overs)**		**141**

Francis 13-4-22-2 Browne 12-0-41-2 Constantine 11.3-3-35-5
Neblett 4-1-14-0 Small 7-0-23-1

West Indies 1st innings

G Challenor		b Irvine	25
CA Roach		b Allom	19
MP Fernandes	st Martin	b Longfield	73
WH St Hill	c Longfield	b Irvine	13
JA Small	lbw	b Irvine	5
FR Martin		b Robins	7
LN Constantine		b Allom	1
CR Browne	c Duleepsinhji	b Robins	7
*+RK Nunes	c Duleepsinhji	b Blundell	10
JM Neblett		b Allom	61
GN Francis	not out		4
Extras	(b 22, lb 9, nb 1)		32
Total	**(all out, 94.2 overs)**		**257**

Allom 31.2-5-60-3 Blundell 11-4-44-1 Longfield 14-3-35-1
Irvine 17-2-46-3 Robins 21-5-40-2

Cambridge University 2nd innings

*FJ Seabrook		b Small	27
TC Longfield	not out		42
KS Duleepsinhji		b Constantine	3
MJL Turnbull		b Francis	43
RWV Robins		b Francis	19
BH Valentine		b Constantine	7
WG Morgan		b Constantine	0
MJC Allom	c Nunes	b Small	5
LG Irvine		b Constantine	1
+T Martin		b Small	2
ED Blundell		b Constantine	1
Extras	(lb 2, w 1, nb 2)		5
Total	**(all out, 47.4 overs)**		**155**

Francis 16-2-30-2 Browne 4-1-18-0 Constantine 15.4-1-51-5
Small 12-0-51-3

West Indies 2nd innings (target: 40 runs)

G Challenor	not out		22
MP Fernandes	c Morgan	b Allom	1
WH St Hill	not out		16
Extras	(nb 1)		1
Total	**(1 wicket, 9.5 overs)**		**40**

DNB: CA Roach, JA Small, FR Martin, LN Constantine, CR Browne, *+RK Nunes, JM Neblett, GN Francis.

Allom 4-0-7-1 Blundell 3-0-12-0 Irvine 1-0-9-0
Robins 1.5-0-11-0

MATCH NO. 6

West Indies in England, 1928

elty of the presence of coloured men playing on a cricket field in England", and indicated that before the tour began there had been much comment that the blacks would go on to the field "without boots and in a very sparse attire". W.L.A. Coleman, surveying the sociological contours of the tour, wrote in *The Cricketer*:

"Apparently the coloured members of the team were much impressed with England and they indicated that in the West Indies the question was being asked as to whether white and coloured cricketers should play together in the same team. It had been the form to allow only white cricketers to play in cup and inter-colonial matches in the West Indies and the *BOP* editor ventured to suggest that 'on the return home, many of the islands must have found themselves in a very awkward position over the matter. If, for instance, any of the coloured players are good enough to represent the team in an international match, it is difficult to see how they can be refused opportunities of playing at home.' This throws interesting light on the prevailing attitudes in the West Indies and how, at the time, their cricket was dominated by the whites. The manager indicated that the coloured players had apparently 'very quickly fallen into English ways' and that 'they gave no trouble whatever during the tour. Indeed, they lived in the same hotels and were treated exactly like the white members'. Woods is purported to have said 'what a lot of white people they have got in this country,' when playing at Crystal Palace."

A.E. Morton cartoon on the West Indies defeat at Crystal Palace in the first game of the 1906 tour to England. Cartoons expressing the opinion of West Indian players as inferior, primitive, uncultured figures were prevalent in that period.

The performances of this team were not particularly impressive. It suffered consecutive defeats in its first four county matches, and was slaughtered in the sixth game against Gloucestershire, whose first innings total of 619 included three centuries and a partnership of 201 made in an hour. In one over, Jessop, who scored 157, struck six fours,

THE 1928 ARCHIVES

CAMBRIDGE PUT IN

THE RETURN OF K. S. DULEEPSINHJI

The wicket at Cambridge on Saturday was again in favour of the bowlers, and, in the course of a full day's play, the scoring was comparatively low. The West Indies' visit attracted a good crowd to the University ground, and, for the most part, the interest was well maintained, although during the last hour the visiting batsmen did not give the impression of a very formidable combination, as their display against the University slow bowling was anything but confident.

There were three changes in the Cambridge team from that which was beaten by Nottinghamshire, examinations claiming J.T. Morgan, E.T. Killick, and N.G. Wykes; and whilst K.S. Duleepsinhji made a very welcome first appearance of the season, the eleven was completed by the inclusion of W.G. Morgan and B.H. Valentine. Duleepsinhji played easily the best innings of the day, and his form was most assuring.

The wicket looked a perfect one, but the West Indies captain, on winning the toss, decided to put the University in to bat, and although his policy seemed to be justified during the early stages, as the day proceeded it was doubtful whether any real advantage was gained, as no big scores were made, and when stumps were drawn the visitors, with three wickets to fall, were 18 runs behind the Cambridge total.

Withoug Longrigg, J.T. Morgan, Wykes or Killick, the University captain was placed in a somewhat unenviable position as to how to open his batting, and it rather seemed that he sacrificed himself by going in first with Longfield, as it was abundantly proved during the past two seasons that Seabrook himself is not an ideal opening batsman.

Both were soon beaten, but then Duleepsinhji and Turnbull settled down to some confident batting, and in little more than an hour they had added 51 when Turnball was sent back by what appeared to be an unfortunate decision.

Duleepsinhji remained for an hour and three-quarters, making some nice strokes, although, curiously enough, he never got one through to the boundary; but it was a most invaluable and encouraging display, full of confidence. Robins had a merry innings, once getting three successive deliveries from Constantine to leg for 4. Morgan was the only other batsman to offer any resistance; and Constantine captured the last four Cambridge wickets in the course of 15 deliveries, the innings lasting only two hours 40 minutes.

*–The Times,
Monday, May 28, 1928, Page 5*

WEST INDIES WIN

CAMBRIDGE BEATEN BY NINE WICKETS

The West Indies beat Cambridge University at Cambridge yesterday by nine wickets, the game ending at 20 minutes to 7.

A protracted stand at the opening of the day's play did everything to place the visitors in a strong position. When play was continued they were 18 runs behind with only three wickets to fall. Nunes, one of the not outs, gave no material assistance, and it was a brilliant catch in the slips by Duleepsinhji that dismissed him. A stay of 50 minutes for 10 runs gives an idea of Nunes's slow methods. When Fernandes was joined by Neblett, the University bowling came in for its most severe test.

As on Saturday, Fernandes refused to be bustled, and it was Neblett who forced the pace. This left-handed batsman proved to be the most enterprising of the side, and from the start of his innings he met the attack with complete confidence so that, whereas he was only 65 minutes in reaching his 50, Fernandes, in direct contrast, was batting for early three hours for a similar number. This partnership did everything to seal the fate of the University, as the ninth wicket stand produced 92 runs in 75 minutes. Fernandes lost his wicket when, in reaching out, the ball rebounded from the wicket-keeper's gloves on to the stumps. As he was batting for four hours for 72 runs, his performance can call for very little praise, but Neblett, who left directly afterwards, was in for only one and a half hours. The last three wickets added 134, and Cambridge were in a minority of 116.

When the University went in a second time Constantine, although having 25 scored from him out of 35, secured three wickets. Valentine was unfortunate in playing on, but Duleepsinhji and Morgan were clean bowled.

*–The Times,
Tuesday, May 29, 1928, Page 6*

The West Indies team in England in 1906. Back row from left: R.C. Ollivierre, C.S. Morrison, L.S. Constantine, G. Challenor, J.E. Parker, J. Burton, O.H. Layne, C.P. Cumberbatch. Seated (middle row): A. E. Harragin, H.B.G. Austin, P. Goodman, G.C. Learmond. Front: C.K. Bancroft, S.G. Smith.

during which the blacks on the team, according to Warner, "sat down on the ground and shouted with laughter at the unfortunate bowler's discomfiture". In this game they were defeated by an innings and 216 runs. Its best performance was against Surrey, whom they defeated by an innings and 34 runs, with Woods returning figures of seven for 48 and five for 68, and Cox and Ollivierre putting on an opening partnership score of 208 runs. The tour was, however, a major historic occasion for black players, and more importantly, the beginning of modern non-racial West Indies 'international' cricket. All that was left was to consolidate the achievements of this start.

From December 1904 to January 1905, Lord Brackley arranged for a tour by an English team to the West Indies, capturing the spirit of a return bout. While in the region, Lord Brackley was clearly impressed with the improvement in the West Indies game since 1900, and arranged for a second West Indies team to tour England the following summer. He also insisted that the tour be designated first class – with a few second-class fixtures to satisfy reluctant commentators.

The 1906 inter-colonial Challenge Cup competition was held in Trinidad, and as soon as it ended, a selection committee, comprising Messrs. Gail and Belgrave (Demerara), P.A. Goodman and H.A. Cole (Barbados), and A.E. Harragin

THE 1928 ARCHIVES

Ireland v West Indies
College Park, Dublin - 4, 5, 6 June, 1928 (3-day match)

Result: Ireland won by 60 runs
Umpires: Gibbons and O Gorman

Ireland 1st innings
AH Robinson	c Roach	b Small	31
L Bookman		b Griffith	0
TJ MacDonald		b Small	11
*JB Ganly	lbw	b Small	43
JG Heaslip	c Wight	b Griffith	11
TO Jameson	not out		45
+AP Kelly		b Small	0
TGB McVeagh		b Griffith	14
PA Thornton		b Griffith	6
EN Seymour		b Small	3
TH Dixon		b Martin	4
Extras	(b 5)		5
Total	(all out, 53.5 overs)		**173**

Griffith 21-3-65-4 Small 22-4-67-5 Scott 5-1-18-0
Neblett 5-1-15-0 Martin 0.5-0-3-1

West Indies 1st innings
CA Roach	c Ganly	b Dixon	0
MP Fernandes	lbw	b Heaslip	11
FR Martin		b Jameson	56
EL Bartlett	lbw	b Heaslip	22
JA Small	c&b	Jameson	0
CR Browne	c Heaslip	b Dixon	11
WH St Hill	c Seymour	b Dixon	4
*CV Wight	c Bookman	b Seymour	26
JM Neblett	c&b	Jameson	1
OC Scott	lbw	b Seymour	0
HC Griffith	not out		0
Extras	(b 7, lb 2, nb 2)		11
Total	(all out, 61.2 overs)		**142**

Dixon 19-5-34-3 Heaslip 19-3-50-2 Jameson 11.2-4-17-3
Seymour 9-2-26-2 Thornton 3-1-4-0

Ireland 2nd innings
AH Robinson		b Scott	15
L Bookman	c Small	b Scott	31
TJ MacDonald	c Small	b Griffith	1
*JB Ganly	c Small	b Scott	31
TO Jameson		b Scott	5
+AP Kelly	lbw	b Small	3
JG Heaslip		b Small	44
TGB McVeagh	not out		102
PA Thornton	c Fernandes	b Neblett	37
EN Seymour	c&b	Neblett	2
TH Dixon		b Scott	19
Extras	(b 25, b 5)		30
Total	(all out, 95.3 overs)		**320**

Griffith 21-2-73-1 Small 31-7-92-2 Scott 21.3-3-61-5
Neblett 8-0-22-2 Martin 7-1-19-0 Roach 7-1-23-0

West Indies 2nd innings (target: 352 runs)
CA Roach	c McVeagh	b Thornton	71
MP Fernandes	c McVeagh	b Dixon	73
WH St Hill	lbw	b Jameson	9
EL Bartlett	c McVeagh	b Seymour	54
JA Small	c Kelly	b Dixon	10
CR Browne		b Dixon	0
JM Neblett	lbw	b Seymour	1
FR Martin	run out		6
*CV Wight	not out		28
OC Scott	st Kelly	b Jameson	0
HC Griffith	c McVeagh	b Dixon	17
Extras	(b 17, lb 5)		22
Total	(all out, 108.1 overs)		**291**

Dixon 32.1-9-76-4 Heaslip 25-8-57-0 Jameson 27-6-75-2
Seymour 15-5-34-2 Thornton 5-1-15-1 Bookman 4-0-12-0

MATCH NO. 7

West Indies in England, 1928

xiv

WEST INDIES IN ENGLAND, 1906
TOUR RESULTS

Opposition	Dates	Venue	Results
W.G. Grace XI	June 11-12	Crystal Palace	Lost by 247 runs
Essex	June 14-16	Leyton	Lost by 111 runs
Lord Brackley s XI	June 18-20	Lord s	Lost by 2 wickets
Minor Counties	June 21-23	Ealing	Won by 215 runs
Surrey	June 25-26	The Oval	Lost by 10 wickets
Wiltshire	Jun. 29-30	Swindon	Lost by 86 runs
Hampshire	July 2-4	Southampton	Lost by 6 wickets
South Wales	July 9-10	Cardiff	Won by 278 runs
Kent	July 12-1	Catford	Lost by an innings and 14 runs
MCC	July 16-17	Lord s	Lost by 6 wickets
Derbyshire	July 23-25	Derby	Lost by 6 wickets
Scotland	July 23-25	Edinburgh	Won by 4 wickets
An England XI	July 26-28	Blackpool	Drawn
Durham/ Northumberland	July 30-Aug 1	Sunderland	Won by 145 runs
Yorkshire	Aug 6-8	Harrogate	Won by 262 runs
Leicestershire	Aug 6-8	Leicester	Lost by 24 runs
Norfolk	Aug 10-11	Norwich	Won by an innings and 118 runs
Nottinghamshire	Aug 13-15	Nottingham	Drawn
Northamptonshire	Aug 16-18	Northampton	Won by 115 runs

Overall results - Lost 10 games; Won 7 games; Drew 2 games.

and G.C. Learmond (Trinidad) met at the Queen's Park Cricket Club to select the West Indies team for the tour. The 14-member team chosen was considered an improvement upon the 1900 team, more balanced and stronger in each department. This time the blacks were not in the minority.

The English cricket press welcomed the team on arrival at Southampton on Monday 4 June, but remained divided throughout the tour on its designation as a first-class outfit.

An insightful assessment of the tour by Gerry Wolstenholme in *The West Indies Tour of England, 1906, (see above chart)* leaves no doubt that for most English spectators and officials the tour revealed two faces of empire and imperial ideology. On one side, it was necessary to encourage the colonials in a paternal sort of way, even if to put them in their subordinate place by defeating them.

THE 1928 ARCHIVES

IRELAND v. WEST INDIES

Although the wicket was in perfect order, Ireland were all dismissed for 173 in their match against the West Indies, which was begun at Collett Park, yesterday, and at the close of play the visiting side had scored 100 runs for the loss of six wickets. Only Jameson, playing with freedom and confidence, was able to withstand the West Indies' bowling for any considerable time. He stayed in an hour for his 45 not out, and was principally responsible for the last three wickets adding 38. Small took five wickets for 67 runs. The visitors made a bad start, and had it not been for a strong innings by Martin they might have ended the day in a worse position.

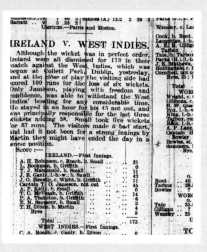

-The Times,
Tuesday, June 5, 1928, Page 6

WEST INDIES IN DUBLIN

The batting failures which have characterized the match between Ireland and the West Indies at Dublin were again in evidence yesterday, for the visitors, continuing 73 runs behind with four wickets in hand, finished their innings 31 runs behind Ireland. Only the left-hander, F.R. Martin, who made 56 in three hours, showed any confidence against the bowling.

Ireland's opening partnership in the second innings gave the side a better start than had been the case on the previous day, but a partial collapse followed, and the captain, J.B. Ganly, again figured prominently in improving the situation. Six wickets had fallen for 92 runs when Ganly left, but then Heaslip and McVeagh added 71 runs for the seventh wicket. Heaslip gave a fine exhibition of free hitting. McVeagh was then associated with Thornton, and they added 106 before the latter fell to a catch at the wicket. McVeagh, who was still unbeaten at the finish with 87 runs to his credit, was responsible principally for his side's commanding lead of 312 with one wicket in hand.

–The Times,
Wednesday, June 6, 1928, Page 7

On the other, given the racial ideology endemic to empire, and the fact that the West Indies team had now acquired an image as a black force despite white leadership, elements of the press found it necessary to cast the contest within a racial paradigm.

The team, on arrival, was invited to dinner by their sponsors, the West Indian Club, at the seemingly appropriate Imperial Restaurant. That official scaffold of imperial hospitality in place, Sir Cavendish Boyle, chairman of the evening's proceedings, toasted the team with language that left no doubt about the perception that West Indies cricketers in England were part of a wider scheme of empire consolidation and promotion. The West Indian guests were cautioned:

"You are to show of what good stuff the children of Britain living in the beautiful climes known as the West Indies are *possessed* ... I hope you pull together, train together, bowl together, bat together, field together for the honour of our sunny homes and add another link in the chain of oneness and wholeheartedness which binds the sons of Great Britain with the children of the greater Britain in that undefeated, age undaunted, whole – our British Empire."

In reply to Sir Cavendish, the West Indies captain indicated, particularly to the press, that his team was a revolutionary exercise in resource organisation as it was drawn from five colonies "thousands of miles apart" and had never played before as one.

The team, like its 1900 predecessor, started off poorly but showed marked improvement as the tour progressed. The first game was against the W.G. Grace XI, on June 11, at Crystal Palace – the same date and venue as the first match in 1900. The West Indies team was trashed by 247 runs. In the second match against Essex they lost by 111 runs, and in the third against Lord Brackley's XI, a second-class game, they lost by two wickets.

Their first defeat sent the press off to work promoting the argument that the West Indians were not a first-class lot, and that the decision to offer them this status was premature. One reporter stated: "The West Indians gave a poor display of fielding. They dropped no less than seven catches (a rather kind estimate); they did not seem to be able to catch anything except the train to take them home". After the game against Lord Brackley's XI, another cricket reporter

THE 1928 ARCHIVES

Middlesex v West Indies
Lord's, London - 9, 11, 12 June, 1928 (3-day match)

Result: West Indies won by 3 wickets
Umpires: JW Day and WR Parry

Middlesex 1st innings

NE Haig		b Small	119
HW Lee	c Martin	b Constantine	7
JW Hearne	c Nunes	b Roach	75
EH Hendren	not out		100
ET Killick		b Francis	6
GOB Allen	run out		4
*FT Mann		b Francis	32
IAR Peebles	not out		0
Extras	(b 2, lb 4, nb 3)		9
Total	**(6 wickets declared, 115.5 overs)**		**352**

DNB: FJ Durston, +WFF Price, JA Powell.

Francis 35.5-4-107-2 Browne 11-2-21-0 Constantine 20-1-77-1
Small 29-5-72-1 Martin 13-0-30-0 Roach 7-0-36-1

West Indies 1st innings

G Challenor	c Hendren	b Durston	23
CA Roach	c Lee	b Durston	0
MP Fernandes	c Hearne	b Allen	29
WH St Hill	c Hendren	b Peebles	5
EL Bartlett	st Price	b Powell	13
FR Martin	not out		26
LN Constantine		b Peebles	86
JA Small	c Hendren	b Haig	7
*+RK Nunes		b Durston	17
CR Browne	c Allen	b Durston	0
GN Francis	lbw	b Haig	1
Extras	(b 18, lb 3, nb 2)		23
Total	**(all out, 89.4 overs)**		**230**

Durston 21-10-16-4 Haig 24.4-7-32-2 Hearne 11-4-25-0
Peebles 18-2-51-2 Allen 8-2-43-1 Powell 7-1-40-1

Middlesex 2nd innings

HW Lee		b Constantine	15
GOB Allen	c&b	Francis	7
JW Hearne	lbw	b Small	28
EH Hendren	c Francis	b Constantine	52
NE Haig		b Constantine	5
ET Killick	c Francis	b Constantine	4
*FT Mann		b Small	4
IAR Peebles		b Constantine	0
FJ Durston	not out		9
+WFF Price		b Constantine	3
JA Powell		b Constantine	1
Extras	(b 3, lb 2, nb 3)		8
Total	**(all out, 38.3 overs)**		**136**

Francis 10-3-30-1 Small 11-3-36-2 Constantine 14.3-1-57-7
Martin 3-0-5-0

West Indies 2nd innings (target: 259 runs)

G Challenor		b Haig	33
CA Roach	run out		10
MP Fernandes	c Allen	b Haig	54
WH St Hill		b Durston	5
EL Bartlett	lbw	b Hearne	26
JA Small	c&b	Peebles	5
LN Constantine	c Haig	b Lee	103
FR Martin	not out		1
CR Browne	not out		4
Extras	(b 18)		18
Total	**(7 wickets, 68.4 overs)**		**259**

DNB: *+RK Nunes, GN Francis.

Durston 15-3-32-1 Haig 22-5-80-2 Hearne 15-3-51-1
Peebles 11-2-45-1 Powell 1-0-6-0 Lee 4.4-0-27-1

MATCH NO. 8

West Indies in England, 1928

complained that "all their bowlers are as mild as the weather itself". A caricature showing the West Indian team as represented by a monkey-like figure being spanked by W.G. Grace, appeared in the press. On the whole, the literary image of an African world – black primitives and white masters – was unleashed, in spite of the claim by Jeremiah Coleman, chairman of Surrey, that the "visit tended to create Imperial good fellowship".

The match against the MCC at Lord's on July 16, the tenth of the tour, provided another opportunity for the press to harangue the West Indians. They were defeated by six wickets after giving the home team 87 runs to win. In an article by cricket journalist H.D. Sewell, under the headline, "What is the matter with the West Indian Team?", readers were informed:

"Once again the West Indies have failed to do themselves justice – as a side... It is a most extraordinary thing that the side, as a side, cannot get going in cricketers' phraseology. Is it just all the difference between first and second class, I wonder? I was chatting with one of the Kent XI and he wondered why they did not get more runs. He said their field was badly placed and only the coloured men are good catchers. They are certainly a mysterious side – and I cannot help thinking they may one day do something surprising."

This tour, however, firmly established the concept of a first-class multiracial West Indies team. The working classes had brought their cricket from the gullies of their villages to the international stage. Wherever they went, they had been excellent representatives of the modern game. Thus they had broken the barriers of institutionalised racism and forged the way towards a new democratic ethos.

If, in 1906, the black cricketers sent on tour to England had weakened the force of colonial opposition to social justice for all, the English, in beating the team, were keen to demonstrate their interest in keeping all colonials – black and white – in a subordinate position. A.E. Morton, a popular English cartoonist, did not miss the opportunity to capture the politics of ethnic relations that surrounded the tour.

A cricket postcard which showed a barefooted black girl dressed like a rag doll bowling to a black boy attired as an agricultural labourer entitled "Happy Little Coons" became very popular during and after the tour. The image was distinctly racist and reflected imperial attitudes to blacks who,

THE 1928 ARCHIVES

WEST INDIES AT LORD'S
MIDDLESEX BAT ALL DAY

The West Indies made their second appearance at Lord's on Saturday, when Middlesex kept them in the field all day to score 313 runs for the loss of six wickets.

The score, as scores go in these days, was not an unusually large one on an easy paced wicket, and the West Indies must be credited on the whole with having done quite well on the day's play. Had their fast bowlers been granted that shade of good luck which fast bowlers quite rightly expect but so seldom get, N. Haig would have scored 100 runs less than he did, but the West Indies can console themselves with the knowledge that by allowing Haig to stay in – he was missed twice in the slips very early in his innings – they escaped the pain of a Hearne-Hendren partnership, Hearne being out before his comrade came in. Individually they are, to be sure, hard enough to get out, but when they are in together they are twice as difficult to shift.

It is no depreciation of Haig's valuable innings to say that what the Saturday afternoon crowd enjoyed more than anything was the magnificent fielding of the West Indies team, and if among a thoroughly keen team L.N. Constantine attracted the most favour it must be on the score that the ball followed him round the field. It is doubtful whether at the moment there is a better all-round cricketer in this country than Constantine; he is a match-winning batsman of the most adventurous type; a definitely fast bowler, and as a fieldsman not even Robinson of Yorkshire, has more original ideas of getting a batsman out.

–The Times,
Monday, June 11, 1928, Page 5

THE WEST INDIES AT LORD'S
L.N. CONSTANTINE'S GREAT BATTING

The play in the match between the West Indies and Middlesex at Lord's threatened at one time yesterday to be disastrous to the touring team, but a truly great innings by L.N. Constantine and an eventful half-hour's play at the end of the day left them full of life and hope to fight again to-day. As the game now stands, Middlesex, with two wickets down in their second innings, are 162 runs ahead.

Everything else in the day's play was entirely put in the shade by Constantine's batting, and it is not flattery to remark that when once he was out cricket seemed to be a dreary game. He went in to bat when five wickets were down for 79 runs, against a Middlesex total of 352, with the bowlers no doubt in thoroughly good conceit with themselves; but half an hour of Constantine entirely changed the outlook of the game.

The cricket-going public have been lucky in that these last two touring sides in this country have possessed cricketers such as C.C. Dacre and Constantine. Whether it be Dacre or Constantine who hits the ball harder, or more often, is open to question. Possibly Dacre could make the ball travel off the bat a little more viciously, but no one living could have shown a more pleasurable intent to score off every ball sent down to him than did Constantine yesterday. Moreover, he tried, so far as he could, to adopt the most orthodox, though now frequently unexploited, method of dealing with each particular ball. Some of his scoring strokes were a revelation to those who had forgotten where runs could be made, and memorable in an innings which must rank among the very best played at Lord's this year were the way in which he hit the fast bowling over mid-wicket's head, a remarkable 6 over cover-point's head which landed high up in the new grand stand, and his straight driving of short-pitched balls. Altogether, after all his magnificent fielding on Saturday and the persistent threat of his fast bowling, Constantine established definite claims to be considered an ideal number eight in a World team.

Middlesex continued their innings with the score at 313 for six wickets at 11.15, and at 11.50 the innings was declared closed. Hendren by then had increased his score from 62 to 100, the total having been taken to 352, and I.A.R. Peebles's overnight score of none not out remaining the same. The West Indies started badly, losing C. Roach in the third over of the innings, but G. Challenor and M.P. Fernandes were still in at the luncheon interval, and the score afterwards had been taken to 39 before Challenor was caught in the slips.

–The Times,
Tuesday, June 12, 1928, Page 7

This cricket postcard of a barefooted black girl dressed like a rag doll bowling to a black boy attired as an agricultural labourer entitled "Happy Little Coons" became very popular during and after the 1906 tour.

through cricket, were seeking to develop a closer association with the progressive elements of English society.

The game played at Lord's against an MCC Club and Ground XI, however, indicated more significantly the bonds already forged in the emergence of an Anglo-West Indian cricket sensibility. The MCC team included two West Indians – Plum Warner (the captain) and E.L. Challenor, brother of the 18-year-old George Challenor of the West Indies team. In this match, George top scored for the tourists in the first innings with a patient innings of 59 (Cumberbatch also made 59) from a total of 240, and Plum did the honours for the MCC with a polished performance of 87 in a 269 total. Sydney Smith dominated the West Indies bowling with a

THE 1928 ARCHIVES

WEST INDIES WIN
CONSTANTINE'S TRIUMPH

The West Indies, after a match which was a continuous triumph for Constantine, beat Middlesex at Lord's yesterday by three wickets.

Constantine's fielding on the first day, his batting yesterday definitely established his claim to be considered as the most determined match-winning cricketer in the world. It is seldom that the Pavilion at Lord's twice rises to a player in one day; but yesterday Constantine was accorded that honour – and it is a very considerable one – first, before luncheon, when he ratted out the Middlesex batsmen, and towards the end of the match, when he had won the match for his side by a gloriously daring display of batsmanship. If further proof is needed of what he can reasonably be expected to do, the unusually large amount of people who left their work unaccountably early was clear testimony, and he did not fail them. Moreover, it is difficult to see how he will fail his admirers. As a fieldsman he may be inclined impetuously to overrun the ball, as a bowler he may not always be able to persuade batsmen to withdraw so obviously as some Middlesex batsmen did yesterday, and as a batsman he may be deceived by a persistent spin bowler, but his record in the match in question was triumphant. In the first Middlesex innings he saved a quantity of runs, and in the West Indies' first innings he for the first time clearly saved his side from defeat. He followed that by giving his team a chance of winning the game by hitting the stumps five times and getting two other batsmen caught in the slips, and he then rounded off a truly wonderful achievement by scoring 103 runs out of 133 for the sixth wicket, when the balance of play was overwhelmingly against his side – a match of which any cricketer may well be proud, and which the spectators at Lord's were fully appreciative. Such compliment as he was paid by every one at Lord's yesterday, spectators, card-sellers, groundsmen, gatemen and all the others who should have been attending to their particular business, probably not even excluding the umpires and the scorers, and most certainly including the beaten side, was remarkable, but no more than he deserved.

When play was continued in the morning Middlesex were in the comfortable position of being 162 runs ahead with eight wickets yet to fall. Hearne and Hendren seemed well set to avoid any possibility of defeat, but there followed a curious turn in the game. Constantine, bowling from the practice ground end, all but bowled Hendren and hit him a wicked blow on the chest in one over. He was taken off, and J.A. Small, who relieved him, did the necessary by sending back Hearne leg-before-wicket. N. Haig then came in, and the West Indies captain very wisely put Constantine on again, this time at the Pavilion end. That decision by R.K. Nunes won the match for his side. Constantine bowled as a fast bowler will do when his tail is up, and Middlesex were all out for 136, and the West Indies required no more than 259 runs to win the match.

After luncheon G. Challenor and M.P. Fernandes, keeping well apace with the clock, for a time established a winning mood, but when at 63 Challenor was bowled the game was apparently nearly won by Middlesex. W. St. Hill was also soon out, and although the diminutive E. L. Bartlett played courageously and attractively, five wickets were down with 138 runs still required for victory.

Fernandes, however, had in the meantime been batting most surely, and no enthusiastic laudation of Constantine must be allowed to belittle what he, too, did for his side. He, in fact, never looked like getting out, and while the crowd stood on their seats to cheer Constantine's audacious hitting, contented himself with playing well within himself and taking the runs as they came along. The running between the wickets of this pair was in itself an education.

Constantine, like all batsmen with a quick brain, is very sure of his own runs, and he is also amazingly quick in the backing up of the striker. A difficult man to run out. Unfortunately this pair, who had done so well by their side, were not together when the winning was made, Constantine being out first, with only five runs more required, and Fernandes following before another of those five runs had been scored.

–The Times,
Wednesday, June 13, 1928, Page 6

L.N. Constantine

haul of five wickets for 78 runs. The West Indies were bundled out for a meagre 115 runs in the second innings, leaving the MCC a mere 87 runs for victory. These runs were made for the loss of three wickets.

Smith had impressed throughout the tour and was invited by Northamptonshire to join their club. He did so and became the first player for the county to score 1,000 runs in a season, and also the first to do the double. He captained the team in 1913-14 but after a total of 117 games with the club, emigrated to New Zealand where he played with Auckland. Charles Ollivierre, the Vincentian star of the 1900 tour, had also opted to play county cricket, and with Smith, constructed the early foundation on which West Indian cricketers would build their monuments within the park of English county cricket.

Plum, in 1900, had foreseen these developments in West Indies cricket, and his disappointment that the West Indies were not granted Test status until 1928, spoke to the potency of the wider imperial agenda to which he was a critical subscriber.

His vision, however, was not born purely of intellectual insight. Rather, it had to do with his earlier exposure to West Indies players as a member of Lord Hawke's team during the tour of 1896-97, particularly to his fellow Trinidadians.

Though Plum was the outstanding batsman of Hawke's team, falling short of 1,000 runs by 16, he had considerable difficulty with the black Trinidadian pacemen, J. Woods and C.P. Cumberbatch. He also had problems with Clifford Goodman, the white Barbadian pacer. In these three men, the West Indies had as good a pace attack as any, and Plum had recognised their importance to the West Indian cause.

White Batsmen, Black Bowlers

The success of Woods and Cumberbatch was the barometer by which West Indians came to measure their suitability for first-class cricket. C.L.R. James had noted that with no opportunities both men had made themselves into bowlers whom most English counties would have been glad to have. Plum Warner did not fare very well against them. He got to 70 before falling to Cumberbatch in his first innings against the pair, and in his next three innings Cumberbatch had him

THE 1928 ARCHIVES

Yorkshire v West Indies
Bramall Lane, Sheffield - 13, 14, 15 June, 1928 (3-day match)

Result: Match drawn
Umpires: RD Burrows and J Moss

Yorkshire 1st innings

P Holmes	c Roach	b Francis	13
H Sutcliffe	c Constantine	b Griffith	24
E Oldroyd		b Francis	23
M Leyland		b Griffith	23
W Barber	c Challenor	b Griffith	6
A Mitchell	c&b	Constantine	18
+A Wood		b Francis	25
E Robinson	c Small	b Griffith	30
W Rhodes	lbw	b Griffith	0
*WA Worsley	not out		7
KA Lister-Kaye		b Griffith	6
Extras	(lb 3, nb 1)		4
Total	(all out, 75.4 overs)		179

Francis 22-7-51-3   Griffith 18.4-5-46-6   Constantine 20-7-44-1
Small 11-1-24-0   Martin 4-1-10-0

West Indies 1st innings

CA Roach	not out		15
G Challenor	c Oldroyd	b Robinson	1
MP Fernandes	c Holmes	b Lister-Kaye	16
LN Constantine		b Robinson	6
EL Bartlett	not out		15
Extras	(lb 2, nb 1)		3
Total	(3 wickets, 26 overs)		56

DNB: *CV Wight, GN Francis, HC Griffith, EA Rae, JA Small, FR Martin.

Lister-Kaye 13-2-30-1   Robinson 11-4-18-2   Rhodes 2-0-5-0

YORKSHIRE v. WEST INDIES

The match between Yorkshire and the West Indies at Bramall Lane, Sheffield, was completely spoiled by rain, only five hours' play being possible – 2¼ on the Wednesday and 2¾ yesterday. Starting at 2 o'clock Yorkshire in an hour and three-quarters increased their score from 94 for four wickets to 179. It not infrequently happens that a man who is not played for his batting plays more attractive cricket than one who is. Wood yesterday continually brought off strokes that Mitchell did not even attempt. The wicket was too soft again for the West Indies fast bowlers, but Griffith and Francis were bowling a length that gave Oldroyd and Mitchell some sort of excuse for their melancholy innings. At 96 Oldroyd was beaten by a length ball off Francis that came in a bit, and of the next 26 runs 25 were scored by Wood. He hit five boundaries, one lucky one through the slips, and four by hard clean strokes that sent the ball exactly where he wished it to go. Had he not hit over and across a ball that pitched at the foot of the middle stump the fast bowlers would probably have had to suffer the indignity of having to put a man out by the sightscreen. Robinson, to the delight of all the Yorkshire men, made the top score of the innings, but wickets were always falling regularly, and nine were down for 167. In putting on 12 runs for the last wicket Captain Worsley made the most remarkable stroke of the innings, a pull off a good length ball from Francis, and K. Lister-Kaye the best, a straight drive off Griffith that was at the Pavilion rails before anyone had time to move.

The West Indies, going in at 4.15, quickly lost G. Challenor, a batsman who is going to be most important to them in the Test Matches, caught at square leg off a bad ball that he did not get hold of. Showers of rain interrupted play for over 40 minutes, and C. Roach and M.P. Fernandes did not go on with their innings until nearly 5.30.

–The Times,
Saturday, June 16, 1928, Page 6

MATCH NO. 9

West Indies in England, 1928

twice for small scores. The pity was that only Woods was able to go to England, for Cumberbatch would surely have succeeded. During his tour, Lord Hawke had said that a team of West Indian cricketers was good enough to play against the English counties, and on this hint a tour was arranged.

The Fight for Test Status

Plum Warner was swimming against the tide in his effort to promote the West Indies to Test status. The 1900 tour was not granted first-class status, and though the 1906 tour had been elevated, there remained racial attitudes within the English cricket establishment that saw West Indian players as inferior and inadequate. The racism at the heart of the British Empire had been demonstrated on the cricketing field much earlier. The first Australian tour to England was in 1868, but this was a team of Aboriginals, put together by an Englishman, Charles Lawrence, their coach and manager. They were not described as the Australian team, as blacks were not allowed by white colonials to represent the colony. The

Plum Warner

THE 1928 ARCHIVES

Minor Counties v West Indies
County Ground, Exeter - 16, 18, 19 June, 1928 (3-day match)

Result: Minor Counties won by 42 runs
Umpires: Painter and Tyler

West Indies 1st innings
G Challenor		b Hazelton	7
CA Roach	c Franklin	b Dynes	92
MP Fernandes		b Hazelton	4
EL Bartlett	c Lockett	b Dynes	31
JA Small	st Franklin	b Dynes	10
FR Martin	c Franklin	b Lockett	81
LN Constantine	lbw	b Relf	5
CV Wight		b Hazelton	11
*+RK Nunes	lbw	b Hazelton	0
HC Griffith	run out		4
GN Francis	not out		12
Extras	(b 18, lb 11, nb 3)		32
Total	**(all out, 96.5 overs)**		**289**

Hazelton 30-9-80-4   Dynes 19-5-43-3   Heathcoat-Amory 10-0-32-0
Lockett 10.5-2-3-   Pitchford 4-0-9-0   Miles 7-2-16-0
Relf 16-4-44-1

Minor Counties 1st innings
HWF Homer	c&b	Constantine	11
WT Cook	c Small	b Francis	10
L Horridge		b Francis	2
E Dynes		b Francis	1
A Lockett		b Griffith	22
WB Franklin		b Constantine	0
RR Relf	c Wight	b Griffith	21
HP Miles		b Griffith	2
H Pitchford		b Griffith	24
EW Hazelton		b Griffith	0
J Heathcoat-Amory	not out		0
Extras	(b 8, lb 5, nb 2)		15
Total	**(all out, 35.2 overs)**		**108**

Francis 15-3-36-3   Griffith 6.2-1-18-5   Constantine 14-3-39-2

Minor Counties 2nd innings (following on)
HWF Homer	c Roach	b Francis	1
WT Cook	c Wight	b Francis	12
L Horridge		b Constantine	15
E Dynes		b Constantine	9
A Lockett	c Small	b Griffith	154
WB Franklin	c Griffith	b Small	33
RR Relf	c Constantine	b Francis	0
HP Miles	c Constantine	b Griffith	61
H Pitchford	run out		12
EW Hazelton	not out		0
J Heathcoat-Amory		b Griffith	2
Extras	(b 14, lb 13)		27
Total	**(all out, 70.1 overs)**		**326**

Francis 19-3-81-3   Griffith 18.1-2-72-3   Constantine 18-2-85-2
Small 9-1-46-1   Martin 6-1-15-0

West Indies 2nd innings (target: 146 runs)
G Challenor		b Relf	4
CA Roach	lbw	b Hazelton	5
MP Fernandes	c Lockett	b Hazelton	6
EL Bartlett	c Franklin	b Hazelton	0
JA Small	c Hazelton	b Relf	15
FR Martin	run out		14
LN Constantine	c Horridge	b Hazelton	14
CV Wight		b Lockett	5
*+RK Nunes	not out		16
HC Griffith		b Hazelton	0
GN Francis	lbw	b Hazelton	11
Extras	(b 4, lb 6, nb 3)		13
Total	**(all out, 35.5 overs)**		**103**

Relf 8-4-25-2   Lockett 8-3-14-1   Heathcoat-Amory 2-0-6-0
Hazelton 17.5-5-45-6

MATCH NO. 10
West Indies in England, 1928

team did reasonably well, winning 14 of the 47 matches: 19 were drawn and 14 lost.

Ten years later, when the Australian side visited England, it was an all-white outfit. The colony had been granted Test status the previous year, in 1877, and the first official Test was played between the two teams at Melbourne. Likewise, the white South Africans were granted Test status in 1889 when England opposed them at Port Elizabeth. But in their 1894 Test tour of England, the white South Africans excluded the black cricketing genius Krom Hendriks because they did not wish to play with or against blacks. The English understood and accepted their policy as consistent with their own thinking and sense of imperial order.

White Barbadians and black Trinidadians were the core of post-war efforts to raise cricket standards in order to secure Test status for the West Indies. Arrangements were made in 1919 for a competition between the two colonies to begin the following year. This contest provided the opportunity for both new and experienced players to perform before local fans, and to build social relations.

Performances were predictable. Barbados scored 623 for five in one match, Percy Tarilton making an extraordinary 304 not out in less than two days. W. St. Hill from Trinidad emerged as a star batsman, but it was J.A. Small who stood out as their most improved player, shifting his focus from medium-fast bowling to middle-order batting.

Challenor and Tarilton were the leading opening batsmen in the West Indies. Unlike Challenor, Tarilton was a patient and cautious stroke-maker whose first instinct was defensive play. But like Challenor, he was a child prodigy. A middle-class white boy from rural Barbados, he attended the Lodge School and played in the first division in the Challenge Cup for his school at age 11. By the time he was 16 he was already one of the best opening batsmen in Barbados. His 304 not out against Trinidad set a Barbadian first-class record which was only broken in 1944 by Frank Worrell. Throughout the 1920s, he and Challenor battered West Indian bowlers. The Trinidadians especially, bore the brunt of their aggression on several occasions, particularly in the 1927 season when the pair put on a 292 partnership. In 1923, on the tour to England he was already 38 and past his best, but his 109 not out against Nottinghamshire represented his considerable skill.

MINOR COUNTIES WIN
HAZELTON BOWLS WELL

The Minor Counties beat the West Indies at Exeter yesterday by 42 runs, the end coming shortly after 3.45. This is the tourists' first defeat in England. The West Indies had the worst of the weather, but it would take considerably more than that to detract from the merit of the Minor Counties' victory.

Rain in the night and in the morning prevented any play before 2.15. The Exeter pitch dries easily and quickly, but for all that it was by no means a comfortable wicket on which to continue an innings broken overnight with the score at 18 for three wickets. The ball was inclined to jump up dangerously, and two of the first three wickets fell through the batsmen's fractional lateness in getting their bats out of the way of good length balls that rose straight to the shoulder of the bat. J.A. Small, who went in with M.P. Fernandes, had an adventurous over from Relf, in the course of which he placed one ball cleverly through the slips for two, hit a four, hit another four round to long leg, yet another four through the slips – this time a lucky one – and was then caught at first slip. W.E. Hazelton then took two wickets, getting Fernandes and L.N. Constantine caught in the slips. That made the score 58 for six, and ten runs later C.V. Wight played over a well pitched-up ball from Lockett and was bowled.

At 78 came the real turning point of the innings. F.R. Martin, batting as though he only wanted someone to stay in with him to win the match, was run out ambling quietly up the pitch for the third run of an overthrow. Martin had obviously no thought of danger in his mind, but in the umpire's opinion W.B. Franklin had the bails off before Martin arrived. H.C. Griffith was bowled next ball, but R.K. Nunes, always a formidable No. 9, and G. Francis added 25 gallant runs for the last wicket before Francis was out leg-before-wicket to a ball that the batsman tried to hit to square leg.

–The Times,
Wednesday, June 20, 1928, Page 7

—*The Times, Wednesday, May 23, 1928, Page 7*

4.

Campaign for Test Status

To some extent, the immediate post-war matches were trials for the upcoming 1923 tour to England. While for blacks the selection process was far from satisfactory, it was understood generally that performances in these games would constitute the basis for inclusion in the touring party. All the talk was about the possibility of Test status being awarded, and players had reason to believe that tour results would be the determining factor. When the side was declared in early 1923, there were few surprises. The team was selected on a quota system. This was an established West Indian method. It made the selection process predictable, but flawed on the basis of merit not always being upheld as first principle. H.B.G. Austin, as expected, was to carry the side, and comments that he was over 40 and thus too old were pushed aside by the widespread recognition that he was still one of the most reliable batsmen in the region.

The other Barbadians chosen were G. Challenor, H.W. Ince, P.H. Tarilton, and G. Francis. From Guiana, came C.R. Browne, and Trinidad provided G. John, V. Pascall, G.A. Dewhurst, L. Constantine and J. Small. Jamaica sent out J.K. Holt, R.K. Nunes and R. Phillips. The little known George Francis of Barbados was chosen over the feared Herman Griffith to bowl the new ball with John on the recommendation of the captain, a decision that surprised spectators. Learie Constantine, whose father, Lebrun, had been a pioneer in the 1900 and 1906 tours, was regarded as a genuine all-rounder and brilliant fielder. Altogether, the team was expected to perform at the highest level – certainly beating most county sides and supporting the argument for West Indies Test status.

THE 1928 ARCHIVES

First Test - England v West Indies

Lord's, London, England - 23, 25, 26 June, 1928
England won by an innings & 58 runs

England 1st innings
H Sutcliffe	c LN Constantine	b GN Francis	48
C Hallows	c HC Griffith	b LN Constantine	26
GE Tyldesley	c LN Constantine	b GN Francis	122
WR Hammond		b LN Constantine	45
DR Jardine	lbw	b HC Griffith	22
*APF Chapman	c LN Constantine	b JA Small	50
VWC Jupp		b JA Small	14
MW Tate	c CR Browne	b HC Griffith	22
+H Smith		b LN Constantine	7
H Larwood	not out		17
AP Freeman		b LN Constantine	1
Sundries	BY: 6 LB: 19 NB: 2 WD: 0 PN: 0		27
Total	**RR: 3.19 runs/6 balls**		**401**

FoW: 1-51, 2-97, 3-174, 4-231, 5-327, 6-339, 7-360, 8-380, 9-389, 10-401

GN Francis 25-4-72-2   HC Griffith 29-9-78-2   LN Constantine 26.4-9-82-4
CR Browne 22-5-53-0   JA Small 15-1-67-2   FR Martin 8-2-22-0

West Indies 1st innings
G Challenor	c H Smith	b H Larwood	29
FR Martin	lbw	b MW Tate	44
MP Fernandes		b MW Tate	0
*+RK Nunes		b VWC Jupp	37
WH St Hill	c DR Jardine	b VWC Jupp	4
CA Roach	run out		0
LN Constantine	c H Larwood	b AP Freeman	13
JA Small	lbw	b VWC Jupp	0
CR Browne		b VWC Jupp	10
GN Francis	not out		19
HC Griffith	c H Sutcliffe	b. P Freeman	2
Sundries	BY: 13 LB: 6 NB: 0 WD: 0 PN: 0		19
Total	**RR: 2.12 runs/6 balls**		**177**

FoW: 1-86, 2-86, 3-88, 4-95, 5-96, 6-112, 7-123, 8-151, 9-156, 10-177

H Larwood 15-4-27-1   MW Tate 27-8-54-2   AP Freeman 18.3-5-40-2
VWC Jupp 23-9-37-4

West Indies 2nd innings
G Challenor		b MW Tate	0
FR Martin		b WR Hammond	12
MP Fernandes	c WR Hammond	b AP Freeman	8
*+RK Nunes	lbw	b VWC Jupp	10
WH St Hill	lbw	b AP Freeman	9
CA Roach	c APF Chapman	b MW Tate	16
LN Constantine		b AP Freeman	0
JA Small	c WR Hammond	b VWC Jupp	52
CR Browne		b AP Freeman	44
GN Francis	c DR Jardine	b VWC Jupp	0
HC Griffith	not out		0
Sundries	BY: 10 LB: 5 NB: 0 WD: 0 PN: 0		15
Total	**RR: 2.27 runs/6 balls**		**166**

FoW: 1-0, 2-22, 3-35, 4-43, 5-44, 6-44, 7-100, 8-147, 9-147, 10-166

MW Tate 22-10-28-2   AP Freeman 21.1-10-37-4   VWC Jupp 15-4-66-3
WR Hammond 15-6-20-1

MATCH NO. 11

West Indies in England, 1928

George Francis bowling against Surrey in 1923.

The team performed reasonably well. The batting failed, though glimpses of brilliance were seen from time to time. The bowling was impressive, occasionally superb, and brought respectability to the overall performance. Sympathisers blamed the weather by drawing attention to the often wet and cold conditions. But this was hardly a satisfactory explanation. George Challenor did consistently well because he was a player of considerable class.

The team returned to the West Indies in triumph. The popular calypso refrain "see the conquering heroes come" was known across the region, and for the first time, cricketers began to assume the identity as popular symbols of a nation imagined. Challenor with the bat, Francis and John with the ball, and Constantine with bat *and* ball, were transported to a central place within the West Indian imagination. They had gone to England, mastered conditions and counties, and had shown a still sceptical public that West Indies cricket had reached the platform of the station.

THE 1928 ARCHIVES

THE WEST INDIANS
TEST TRIAL TEAMS

(FROM OUR CRICKET CORRESPONDENT.)

Since the War, the horrors of winter in England have regularly been in some degree relieved by opportunities of reading in the newspapers accounts of cricket matches played by English teams touring in the West Indies. Some of the tours have been organized by the M.C.C., some by private enterprise. If memory serves, no touring party has returned with an unbeaten record. In fact, on their own wickets and in their own climate the West Indian cricketers have had the better of their guests. Therefore, the competent authority has done no more than justice to their proved ability by offering them the chance to include three Test matches in their programme for the current season at home. A Cambridge man would say that this action has placed the West Indians in Class I., Division II., of the Cricket Tripos.

At the moment there is no reason to expect that before Mr. Nunes and his party embark on their return journey they will have proved themselves worthy to join the Australians and the South Africans in Class I., Division I. They escaped defeat for the first month of the tour. But last week they failed rather ominously in Ireland. Some excuse may be offered for their failure. All the reserve players of the party were called upon to take part in what Irishmen will surely describe as the International Match. But when everything has been said in extenuation of the Dublin fiasco, no reasonable person can expect that England will fail where Ireland has succeeded.

THE AUSTRALIANS OF 1888

It must, however, be remembered that funny things have happened in Test matches, particularly when the manifestly weaker side has possessed a pair of occasionally devastating bowlers. Australia sent in 1888 a side which proved to be much weaker than any of its predecessors. The weather that year was dreadful. The Australians suffered from it so much that there were occasions when they were hard put to it to find 11 men capable of taking the field. Mr. Percy M'Donnell, their captain, was quite disheartened by the performances of his side in many of their earlier matches, and by the smallness of the gates which they attracted. Current gossip said that he seriously contemplated the advisability of cutting losses and taking the next boat back to Australia. But he had Turner and Ferris to bowl for him, and decided to carry on at least until the Lord's Test match had been played.

The wicket on the occasion was "made" for Turner and Ferris, who won the game for Australia. The prestige of that victory, combined with an improvement in the weather, relieved the anxieties of the captain and his manager. During the remainder of the tour a satisfactory measure of success was achieved, and at the end of it the accounts showed a balance of profit over loss. Again, in 1890, the Australian team might without impropriety be described as consisting of Turner, Ferris, Blackham, and eight others. Probably it was weaker than that of 1888. But in the Test match at the Oval, on another Turner and Ferris wicket, England ought to have been beaten, W. G. ought to have "bagged a brace" for the first and only time in his life, and how the last dozen runs were collected goodness alone knows.

It is possible to discover some points of similarity between Mr. Nunes' West Indian team and those two Australian teams of the long ago. Its record of achievement up to date is neither more nor less impressive than were theirs at the corresponding stages of their tours. Like them, it will be opposed to an England team seven — some would say eight – of whose constituents choose themselves. That is an ominous fact, the significance of which has no doubt been fully appreciated by our visitors.

Thirdly, the West Indians' sole chance of victory is based on the possibility that a pair of bowlers – and for this purpose a pair contains three units – will twice go through the batting strength of England. That chance is the more remote because the men capable of following the example set by Turner and Ferris depend on pace through the air and off the pitch. Lord's is not nowadays the fast bowlers' Paradise that it was when a famous Yorkshireman, playing in Gentlemen and Players match, remarked that it was no good running a short run to get away from Brearley if you had to face Knox. In those days a wicket-keeper standing back to a fast bowler at Lord's had a most unpleasant task. The ball came to him at constantly varying heights.

Of recent years one has seldom seen a wicket-keeper at Lord's yorked on the second bounce by a ball which has skidded off the pitch. In fact, he has no more difficulty there than at the Oval in determining the exact place at which to stand in order to save the byes. Very possibly the West Indian fast bowlers will enjoy brief spells of startling success in their first Test match, provided that their slips give them the support which they have hitherto lacked. Certainly each of them will endeavour to show his colleagues what fast bowling really is. But it is not to be expected that their physical exertions and zealous enthusiasm will seriously incommode Hobbs, Sutcliffe, and the rest.

–The Times,
Thursday, June 14, 1928, Page 7

George Challenor batting, 1923.

George Challenor

Challenor was rated a batsman of great class. Perhaps, more than any other player, he established West Indian batsmanship at the world level. But he was already 35 during the 1923 tour. Described as aggressive with a classical style, Challenor also possessed a sound defence. It was for him a splendid tour. He scored eight impressive hundreds, including a forceful 155 not out against Surrey. The other teams against whom he scored centuries were Oxford University, Essex, Northamptonshire, Nottinghamshire, Gloucestershire, Glamorgan and Worcestershire. He scored an extraordinary 1,556 runs on tour, and had an average in first-class matches of 51.86. He then continued his domination of bowling attacks at home. In the 1927 domestic season he hit a magnificent 220 off Trinidad and 105 against Guiana. By this time he was already considered the greatest batsman the West Indies had ever produced. In England, the comment was often heard that the century he struck off Nottinghamshire in his 1906 debut tour, at the age of 18, was among the finest ever played there by a debutant.

THE 1928 ARCHIVES

ENGLAND v. WEST INDIES

SHOCK TACTICS COUNTERED

(FROM OUR CRICKET CORRESPONDENT.)

Circumstances combined to make the start of the first Test Match between England and the West Indies a memorable occasion. The weather was perfect. Each side contained several players of magnetic personalities whose idiosyncrasies are not yet familiar to the general, and never will become stale. And the Committee of the M.C.C. had advertised the event as effectively as economically: they had communicated with the Press the news that 18,000 seats were available for spectators, and that the gates of Lord's would be closed so soon as the number of persons who could see the game in comfort had passed through them. Here it may be remarked that early in the afternoon, when it became obvious that a large part of the Grand Stand was going to remain unoccupied, instructions were given to admit all and sundry to the vacant seats.

This was a discreet and courteous action and the crowd deserved the implied compliment. All day it showed excellent discrimination in its selection of incidents to applaud, and, upon occasion, by refraining even from good words. Uninstructed onlookers, had they been present in force, would have been tempted to display their ignorance during the first two hours of play by applauding ironically the concentration of the batsmen on defence, of the misplaced enthusiasm of the bowlers who appealed for leg-before whenever ball hit pad. The umpires, Braund and Chester, more than once answered these appeals Pepys-like by "making as if they would speak with one on horseback."

Whatever may happen to-day and to-morrow at Lord's, or on other grounds before the season ends, the out-cricket of the West Indians on Saturday indicates that the compliment, which has been paid to them, has not been prematurely offered. During the two hours before luncheon the three fast bowlers, Francis, Constantine, and Griffith, kept Sutcliffe, Hallows, Tyldesley rigorously pegged down. And of the three batsmen Tyldesley alone seemed reasonably certain of his ability to avoid disaster. The bowlers were supported by excitedly enthusiastic fielding, the only blot on which was that, when a short run was taken, the insulted fieldsman would sometimes try to thrown down the wicket before he had picked up the ball.

THE MASTERY OF THE BAT

In the earlier part of the afternoon Tyldesley and Hammond definitely established the mastery of the bat. Jardine also played in a masterly way for a comparatively brief period. Then, with four wickets down for 231, Chapman obviously issued orders for speeding up the pace of the run-getting, and came in himself to show how it should be done. He and Tyldesley put on 96 in 70 minutes, and to achieve that not very startling measure of success they had to take great risks, for the bowlers offered them very few cheap 4's. When the sixth wicket fell at 339 something less than an hour of play time remained, and there were Jupp, Tate, Smith, and Larwood to come. None of these can justly be described as a sticky or uncatholic batsman. But their combined efforts produced no more than 41 runs at the cost of two more wickets.

Even in those old days when, if what we hear in pavilions is true, bowlers really could bowl, the batting was generally the salient feature of a notable day's cricket. Certainly the occasions are now very rare when one leaves the ground, as one did on Saturday, thinking first and foremost of the bowling seen. Nunes, of course, relied mainly on his fast bowlers. He judged their capacity and stamina so nicely that he could constantly employ shock tactics, at least from one end. Constantine is definitely the fastest of them. In fact he alone answers to the definition of a fast bowler as one who cannot bowl a bad length ball provided that he hits ground. On the day Griffith looked the most difficult; his ability to make the old ball swing at 6 p.m. was quite remarkable. A common virtue in the actions of the three declares itself. They all draw themselves up to full height as they reach the crease and brace the left leg firmly against the revolving right arm. This they contrive to do without checking the momentum of a 25-yard run.

D. R. Jardine.   A. P. F. Chapman.

—*The Sporting Chronicle,*
Monday, July 23, 1928, Front Page

–*The Times,*
Monday, June 25, 1928, Page 5

Challenor, they said, was "born rich and batted like a millionaire". Like his captain in 1923, H.B.G. Austin, he was born in Barbados to an upper-class, white, merchant family. He was the youngest of four brothers, all of whom played first division cricket for Wanderers Club. He attended Harrison College, and showed his batting ability before entering his teens. All who saw the young George knew that he was destined for greatness, but there was insufficient exposure to international cricket to develop his outstanding skills. He, nonetheless, flew the West Indian flag, and answered with his bat the questions asked about the ability of the island cricketers to hold their own internationally.

The 1926 tour of an MCC team to the West Indies also served to display the general rule of white batsmanship and black bowling that had guided the development of the first-class game. Austin, Nunes, Tarilton, Challenor, St. Hill and Wight performed well with the bat, and C.R. Browne scored an aggressive, high-speed century against the tourists at Guiana. Constantine symbolised the spirit of West Indian fast bowling and athletic fielding. He was expected to bowl all day while taking up the fielding position at cover-point, and then be ready to produce a swashbuckling innings. By

MCC Team selected to go to Australia in 1924: Back row from left: H. Howell, R.K. Tyldesley, A.P.F. Chapman, S.C. Toone (Manager), N.W. Tate, W.W. Whysall, J.L. Bryan. Middle row: F.E. Wooley, J.W. Hearne, J.W. Douglas, Captain A.E. Gilligan, J.B. Hobbs, E.H. Hendren, H. Strudwick. Front row: R. Kilner, A.P. Freeman, H. Sutcliffe, A. Sandham.

THE 1928 ARCHIVES

ENGLAND v. WEST INDIES
A SAD COLLAPSE

(FROM OUR CRICKET CORRESPONDENT.)

For well nigh a day and a half the West Indians played Test Match cricket as skilfully and as resolutely as the selected of England. On Saturday their bowlers never completely lost the attack, and for the greater part of the day were attacking ferociously. Yesterday Challenor and Martin methodically and resolutely kept up their wickets for two hours, and looked as if they were capable of doubling the term of their occupation. But after luncheon Tate and Larwood, who may have been faint for the lack of it began to bowl with marked increase of fire, and got rid of the two openers in consecutive overs.

Their departure was followed by a regrettable collapse. Tate got another wicket in his next over, and when the slow bowlers came on, rather to save Larwood and Tate from unnecessary fatigue than because the situation required a change of tactics, they enjoyed themselves hugely. Neither Jupp nor Freeman can justly be described as a guileless bowler. But nervous and excited batsmen detected more guile than was actually there. Consequently traps were set with impunity and batsmen fell into them as of set purpose. The spectators, were as bitterly disappointed as the players; for there was no mistaking the fact that the sympathies of the crowd were entirely uninfluenced by patriotism. Possibly Nunes sensed impending disaster. Anyway, he altered the order printed on the card and came in himself at the fall of the third wicket. It would be overflattering to describe him as an extraordinarily accomplished batsman, but he recognizes a half-volley when he sees one, even at Lord's in the course of a Test Match. He played an innings of which he may reasonably be proud. Constantine, the other man who might have done something to save the game, is suffering from reaction after his recent successes. His confidence may be unimpaired; discretion has certainly left him for a while. After he had got himself out by changing his mind in the middle of a stroke and Nunes had hit against the break of a half-volley, the innings was soon over. Unfortunately, the collapse continued when the West Indians went in again, and unless the prophesied rain stops further play there can be but one end to the match.

THE CHRONOLOGY OF THE PLAY

Chapman decided to let Smith and Larwood continue England's incomplete innings, and Constantine saw to it that the end of it should be speedy. In his first over he made a desperate attempt to catch Smith off his own bowling. Smith cocked the ball up only a yard or two in front of him and Constantine's enormous stride got him within inches of reaching it. The next ball sent the off-stump dancing widdershins. Freeman saw Larwood make a few nice strokes before sharing Smith's fate. Constantine had caused the ball to fly rather terrifically. So the chances were that Larwood, bowling from the pavilion end, would be distinctly unpleasant. He did make the short ball rear up straight and when nine runs had been scored he hit Martin on the side of the head. So far from being laid out by the blow the batsman was not seriously discomposed by it. He resumed after a very short interval. His partner, Challenor, played like a great batsman who had temporarily lost his form, and was earnestly endeavouring to recover it by exercise of the sternest self-restraint. Martin, though playing well to leg, was not so sound on the off side and might early have been caught at the wicket off Tate. Chapman evidently believes in changing the bowling early and often. At 16, scored in 35 minutes, he put on Freeman and let Tate change to the pavilion end. Martin made one delightful off-drive off the slow bowler, but the batsmen provided few other incidents of note. Indeed, the inquisitiveness of Tate, who kept hitting the pads at frequent intervals, and the fielding of Jardine provide one's most vivid memories of the pre-luncheon play.

[Photo: Central Press.]

FREEMAN.

—*The Birmingham Mail, Tuesday, July 24, 1928, Page 5*

After the interval, which was prolonged by ten minutes, Larwood bowled just about as fast as Constantine had, and was all round the stumps of both batsmen. Tate also caused the ball to make haste off the pitch, and one which kept low caught Martin in front of his stumps. In the next over Challenor was palpably caught at the wicket. Then the procession began. The first wicket fell at 86, and when ten runs had been added five men were out. Constantine, enthusiastically welcomed by the crowd, made three powerful hits – two of them to unexpected places – and then tamely knocked a shortish ball up to mid-on. The tailenders managed to stay for a while with Nunes and obliged Chapman to call once again on his fast bowlers. They did not do what was wanted; so Jupp and Freeman were reinstated. They finished off the innings precisely at the time set for the tea interval.

–*The Times, Tuesday, June 26, 1928, Page 7*

1928, he had emerged as the global icon of black cricket, the first truly great West Indian superstar. Nonetheless, he took instructions on the field from white men of considerably less talent whose selection often, even as players, could not be argued on the basis of cricketing performance.

The decision to grant the West Indies Test status came in 1928, and in the spring of that year, trial matches were organised in Barbados to pick the team that would play three Tests against the MCC in England during the summer. This was the grand moment for West Indies cricketers. Long overdue, Plum Warner and others argued, but momentous, nonetheless. Some 50 years of touring North America and England, gathering experience and consolidating a first-class team culture, had come to maturity. The MCC finally agreed that the Test encounter was the appropriate context within which to meet the West Indies.

The outstanding success of the 1923 tour to England was a seminal moment in West Indies cricket. More than any other encounter with the English, it provided compelling evidence that the West Indies team was ready for Test cricket status. The determination of the West Indians to do well and settle the matter of achieving Test rank, was obvious to all who had witnessed their performances.

From left: G.H. Hirst, Wilfred Rhodes and Lord Hawkes in 1928.

ENGLAND BEAT THE WEST INDIES
A DELAYED ENDING

(FROM OUR CRICKET CORRESPONDENT.)

The inevitable happened yesterday at Lord's, England beating the West Indies by an innings and 58 runs, but only after an interval whose great length was quite creditable to the tail-end batsmen of the West Indian team. The last four wickets actually put on 122 runs. Of these 23 had been scored on Monday evening by Roach and Small. During the final act of the drama these two and Browne showed no signs of the soul-destroying excitement which, rather than lack of technical skill, had caused their more highly-placed colleagues to collapse.

It may reasonably be deduced that the batting form of the tourists is more truly represented by the stand of Challenor and Martin at the start of the first innings, and by the sound play of Roach, Small, and Browne at the finish of the second, than by the procession of nervous suicides which intervened.

Experience, even an experience for the moment humiliating, is of great value to games-players sufficiently endowed with natural ability to profit by it. That the cricketers from the West Indies answer to this description there can be very little doubt. Therefore it is not to be expected that when the second Test Match is played, at Manchester towards the end of July, history will exactly repeat itself. In the interval some of our county teams may meet with disconcerting shocks.

A TAMER PITCH

The threat of rain was not entirely unfulfilled. A light shower fell just before the hour for continuing play. Its effect was to reduce the liveliness of the Lord's wicket, and make consistently accurate timing of the ball easier than it had been earlier in the match. Roach and Small opened confidently against Freeman and Tate, the latter helped by a strong wind blowing behind him from the Pavilion end. Each batsman played Freeman discreetly and comfortably, and each brought off a delightful drive past cover-point when Tate overpitched.

But Tate's pace off the pitch had its reward. Roach, a trifle late in playing at a length ball, was magnificently caught at second slip. A shorter man than Chapman might have failed to reach the ball. A taller, standing in the presently fashionable attitude of slip-fielders – feet widespread, knees straight – would hardly have touched it. Small and Browne then made the stand of the innings. They played each ball on its merits, and they sorted the balls sent down to them into their proper classes, good, bad, and indifferent, with a most excellent judgment. They brought on Jupp and Hammond for Tate and Freeman, but at first the effect of the change was to speed up the pace of the scoring.

Of the many good strokes played there was one by Browne which, of itself, made the journey to Lord's worth while. Jupp gave him a ball pitched well up on the line of his pads, and breaking back. Aiming at mid-on Browne swung straight batted, and the ball flew with a rather low trajectory into a row of seats half-way up the Mound stand. Small, having completed his 50 with a fine off-drive, was cleverly caught at mid-off. Francis hitting to leg with the modern sweep, not the George Parr drive, skied the pass to Jardine, and Freeman, coming on for Hammond, bowled Browne with one that turned a lot from leg.

CHAPMAN'S LEADERSHIP

The members of the England team individually and collectively did all that was required of them, Chapman, for the second time in two tries, proved that he has something of a genius for captaincy in Test Matches. Not everybody in the ring was as well satisfied with Smith's wicket-keeping as were, it is understood, the bowlers, whose opinion on this subject is the most

Roach

respectable. Lord's can be a horrid ground in dry weather on which to keep wicket. In fact, it is difficult to name a wicket-keeper, other than Oldfield the Australian, who has not since the War at some time, and in some degree, blotted his copybook here.

It seems improbable that the selectors will feel constrained to make many changes in the team for the Manchester match. Indeed, one does not envy them the task of deciding who shall stand down on the Old Trafford ground for Hobbs if he is fit to open the batting once more for England.

–The Times,
Wednesday, June 27, 1928, Page 7

The West Indian team on their arrival in England in 1923.

West Indies cricket, though, had suffered more than that of the English and the Australians by the First World War. Very little first-class cricket was played at home. By the summer of 1919, English county cricket was back in full flight, and the Australians had emerged as a very competitive team by 1921.

When the West Indians arrived in England in 1923, only Harold Austin and George Challenor from Barbados had toured England, yet the team adjusted well to conditions, and delivered superb performances. It was an excellent all-round exhibition; particularly striking were the effectiveness of the pace bowling by George Francis, the out-fielding, and the class batting by Challenor.

In the 1900 tour, the West Indians had played 17 matches, winning just five, losing eight, and drawing four. In 1906, 19 matches were played; they won seven, lost 10 and drew two. In 1923, however, the West Indians won 13 of the 28 matches; lost seven and drew eight.

The high points have remained etched in the annals of English county cricket. In the second match of the tour, for example, the West Indians brushed aside the powerful Sussex team, before defeating the mighty Surrey by ten wickets. With bat and ball the West Indians excelled. The Surrey batsmen had no answer to the pace of George Francis, who intimidated them with a five-wicket haul that

Northamptonshire v West Indies

County Ground, Northampton - 27, 28 June, 1928 (3-day match)

Result: West Indies won by an innings & 126 runs
Umpires: W. Bestwick and W. Cooper

Northamptonshire 1st innings
CN Woolley		b Constantine	7
AG Liddell		b Constantine	15
BW Bellamy	c Griffith	b Constantine	5
JE Timms	c Constantine	b Browne	17
FI Walden		b Constantine	0
ADG Matthews		b Constantine	0
AE Thomas		b Constantine	28
WC Brown		b Browne	13
+GH Johnson	not out		0
JS Nicholson	run out		4
EW Clark		b Constantine	0
Extras (b 8, lb 2, nb 1)			11
Total	**(all out, 38.1 overs)**		**100**

Small 3-0-8-0   Griffith 5-1-17-0   Browne 12-4-19-2
Constantine 18.1-2-45-7

West Indies 1st innings
ELG Hoad	c Johnson	b Clark	3
FR Martin	lbw	b Clark	38
EL Bartlett	lbw	b Clark	0
*+RK Nunes		b Clark	36
G Challenor	c Walden	b Timms	97
JA Small		b Matthews	12
LN Constantine	lbw	b Thomas	107
CR Browne	c Matthews	b Clark	6
EA Rae		b Clark	0
CV Wight	not out		35
HC Griffith	not out		61
Extras	(b 24, lb 11, w 1, nb 3)		39
Total	**(9 wickets declared, 132 overs)**		**434**

Clark 30-12-52-6   Thomas 43-8-117-1   Matthews 32-2-118-1
Nicholson 18-4-63-0   Timms 9-1-45-1

Northamptonshire 2nd innings
CN Woolley		b Constantine	33
AG Liddell	c Rae	b Constantine	6
BW Bellamy		b Constantine	7
JE Timms		b Constantine	56
FI Walden	lbw	b Constantine	0
ADG Matthews	c Rae	b Constantine	0
AE Thomas		b Browne	26
WC Brown	c Hoad	b Small	18
+GH Johnson		b Griffith	24
JS Nicholson	not out		17
EW Clark		b Griffith	14
Extras	(b 1, lb 6)		7
Total	**(all out, 74.4 overs)**		**208**

Griffith 13.4-4-43-2   Browne 14-5-29-1   Constantine 22-4-67-6
Small 16-6-36-1   Martin 9-1-26-0

MATCH NO. 12
West Indies in England, 1928

sent the entire team back for a mere 87 runs.

Throughout the summer, the ferocious, controlled speed of veteran George John, the Trinidadian, paired with the raw hostility of Francis from Barbados, exposed the limitations of English batting as far as pace was concerned. They were a magnificent pair, between them taking 186 wickets (Francis, 96 at 15.32 and John, 90 at 14.68). In the match against Sussex, Francis took 10 wickets, and against Middlesex, he took six for 34 in the first innings. Together, they showed the young Learie Constantine what was expected of him. Learie did well with his 48 wickets as the change bowler, while consistently and aggressively pressing his claim to take the new ball.

Challenor completed the exercise with a swashbuckling 155 not out that established his credentials as one of the finest batsmen in the world. According to Clayton Goodwin, Challenor, by "making 1,895 runs, including eight centuries … became known as the best visiting batsman between

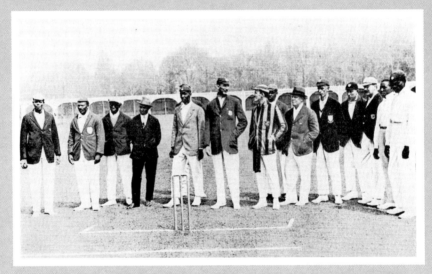

The West Indies team in England, 1923: From left: C.R. Browne, G. John, G.N. Francis, R.L. Phillips, E. Pascall, H.B.G. Austin, R.K. Nunes, J.K. Holt, G. Dewhurst, C.V. Hunter, M.P. Fernandes, G. Challenor, L.N. Constantine, J.A. Small.

Victor Trumper and Donald Bradman".

West Indies cricket was on a high following the 1923 tour. The MCC toured the region in 1925-26 and found that circumstances had changed dramatically since the pre-war tours. Thirteen matches were played; the West Indies won two, the MCC one, and 10 were drawn. When Lord Tennyson's team toured the following winter, it too, was soundly defeated. Seven matches were played; six were

THE 1928 ARCHIVES

WEST INDIES WIN

GREAT ALL-ROUND PLAY OF L.N. CONSTANTINE

The West Indies beat Northamptonshire, at Northampton yesterday, by an innings and 126 runs. This result was due largely to the fine all-round play of L.N. Constantine, who secured 13 wickets in the course of the match, performed the hat trick, and played a three-figure innings.

As had been the case on Wednesday, the Northamptonshire batsmen found the fast bowling of Constantine too much for them. Going in for the second time 334 in arrears, the county had five wickets down for 56 runs, Constantine doing the "hat trick" in the first over following the tea interval by dismissing Woolley, Walden, and Matthews with successive balls.

Earlier in the day the Northamptonshire bowlers had come in for severe punishment, the West Indies increasing their total of 211 for five wickets to 434 for nine, and then declaring. When Constantine who was missed before he had scored, left at 261 he had made 107 out of 146 in 90 minutes, hitting five 6's and 12 4's. Challenor, who was very restrained for some time, afterwards followed Constantine's example, and scored freely off all the bowlers with the exception of Clark, who, in three spells, sent down 30 overs for 52 runs and six wickets. Challenor was batting in all for three hours and 20 minutes, hitting nine boundaries, and after some enterprising batting by Griffith, who obtained no fewer than 13 4's in scoring 61, the innings was declared closed.

Northamptonshire at the interval had scored 56 runs for two wickets, but then came Constantine's "hat trick." Although the position was hopeless, Timms and Thomas batted with such fine resolution that they put on 54 runs, and after they were parted Brown stayed with Timms while 37 were added for the seventh wicket. Timms left at 155, having batted for two hours. He hit one 6 and seven 4's. Johnson was ninth out just before half-past 6. Play went on, however, in order that a definite result might be reached, but Clark and Nicholson defended so stubbornly that Northamptonshire's last wicket did not fall until 7 o'clock. Constantine's record for the match was 13 wickets for 112 runs.

–The Times, Friday, June 29, 1928, Page 7

MCC Team in the West Indies, 1925-26 tour. Standing from left: P. Holmes, W.R.Hammond, E.J. Smith, R. Kilner, C.F. Root. Seated: W.E. Astill, G.C. Collins, The Hon. L.H. Tennyson, The Hon. F.F.G. Calthorpe, H.L. Dales, Captain T.O. Jameson.

drawn, and the West Indies won the series 1-0.

Within this context, the West Indians began putting the necessary systems in place to launch their cricket into Test status. The cricket fraternity met in Bridgetown, Barbados on January 22, 1927, under the chairmanship of L.T. Yearwood. They resolved to establish the West Indies Cricket Board of Control. H.B.G. Austin was appointed President for two years, and H.A. Cuke (Barbados) was the first Secretary. Barbados, British Guiana, Jamaica and Trinidad were allotted two representatives each, and the Leeward and Windward Islands, one each.

The selection process, at the outset, seemed determined to ensure that the first Test team would be the best the region could put on the field at Lord's. The finest West Indian players were assembled at Kensington Oval in Bridgetown for three trial matches under the eyes of the selection panel. It was a process demanding the greatest scrutiny. For the first match, it was decided that Trinidad and Guiana would combine to take on a Barbados and Jamaica XI. St. Hill and Roach booked their passages by scoring 144 and 84 respectively when Trinidad-Guiana amassed 378 runs. The Barbados-Jamaica XI was sent crashing to 59 all out, compliments of an excellent bowling spell by Small, who also booked his trip.

The second match saw no distinguished performances, and the third, between a Barbados Born XI and the Rest of

THE 1928 ARCHIVES

Lancashire v West Indies
Old Trafford, Manchester - 30 June, 2, 3 July, 1928 (3-day match)

Result: Match drawn
Umpires: EF Field and J Hardstaff

Lancashire 1st innings
FB Watson	lbw	b Martin	48
C Hallows	run out		25
GE Tyldesley	lbw	b Constantine	44
JWH Makepeace		b Griffith	7
J Iddon	c Nunes	b Griffith	32
JL Hopwood	run out		0
EA McDonald		b Francis	46
RK Tyldesley		b Constantine	2
*L Green		b Browne	7
+G Duckworth	c Francis	b Browne	1
G Hodgson	not out		6
Extras	(b 12, lb 5)		17
Total	**(all out, 92.4 overs)**		**235**

Francis 19.4-6-30-1 Browne 20-1-56-2 Constantine 14-4-38-2
Griffith 21-2-70-2 Martin 18-7-24-1

West Indies 1st innings
CA Roach	lbw	b Iddon	23
FR Martin		b Hodgson	3
MP Fernandes		b Iddon	7
EL Bartlett	lbw	b RK Tyldesley	7
G Challenor	c RK Tyldesley	b Iddon	26
*+RK Nunes	lbw	b RK Tyldesley	11
LN Constantine		b RK Tyldesley	15
CV Wight		b Hopwood	9
CR Browne	c Hodgson	b McDonald	4
HC Griffith	c Duckworth	b Iddon	0
GN Francis	not out		2
Extras	(lb 1)		1
Total	**(all out, 50.1 overs)**		**108**

McDonald 9.1-2-19-1 Hodgson 8-3-20-1 Iddon 15-5-40-4
RK Tyldesley 12-4-20-3 Hopwood 6-2-8-1

Lancashire 2nd innings
FB Watson	lbw	b Martin	51
C Hallows	not out		49
GE Tyldesley	not out		31
Extras	(b 8, lb 2, nb 3)		13
Total	**(1 wicket declared, 38 overs)**		**144**

DNB: JWH Makepeace, J Iddon, JL Hopwood, EA McDonald, RK Tyldesley, *L Green, +G Duckworth, G Hodgson.

Francis 8-0-39-0 Browne 3-0-9-0 Constantine 12-2-36-0
Griffith 6-2-14-0 Martin 9-1-33-1

West Indies 2nd innings (target: 272 runs)
CA Roach		b RK Tyldesley	82
FR Martin	not out		77
LN Constantine	lbw	b RK Tyldesley	2
MP Fernandes	not out		5
Extras	(b 5, lb 6, nb 1)		12
Total	**(2 wickets, 56 overs)**		**178**

DNB: EL Bartlett, G Challenor, *+RK Nunes, CV Wight, CR Browne, HC Griffith, GN Francis.

McDonald 5-0-19-0 Hodgson 8-1-40-0 Iddon 16-5-50-0
Hopwood 8-3-15-0 Watson 4-0-20-0 RK Tyldesley 15-6-22-2

MATCH NO. 13
West Indies in England, 1928

the West Indies, made the point about the regional standing of Barbados. In a high-scoring affair, Hoad, 153, Bartlett, 93 not out, and Tarilton, 93 and 71, reflected the might of the Barbadians. Wight's 119 not out, and good performances also from Rae, Small and St. Hill indicated the wealth of talent available to the selectors.

Tarilton, however, was considered too old for the tour, and was excluded when the team was announced on February 24, 1928. No spinner was included in the team, and no wicket keeper of known distinction, strange omissions for a tour to England that included three very fast bowlers.

On the 1906 tour of England, the captain was H.B.G. Austin (seated at centre). This was the second time a West Indian team had visited England. George Challenor is on the far left, and Lebrun Constantine, the father of Learie, is second from left, middle row.

The MCC in the West Indies, 1930 tour.
Back row from left: J. Hardstaff (scorer), L.E.G. Ames, G.T.S. Stevens, W. Voce, W.E. Astill, R.H. Mallett (Manager). Seated middle row: G. Gunn, E.P. Hendren, N.E. Haig, Captain The Hon. F.F.G. Calthorpe, W. Rhodes, A. Sandham, R.E.S. Wyatt. Front: L.S. Townsend and J. O'Connor.

WEST INDIES AT OLD TRAFFORD
ROACH AND MARTIN IN FORM

The match between Lancashire and the West Indies ended at Old Trafford in a draw yesterday. Lancashire declared just before 3 o'clock, leaving the West Indies 272 to make in a little under three hours. They did not succeed in bringing off another victory like that against Middlesex, but C.A. Roach and F.R. Martin, in scoring 135 runs for the first wicket, gave the crowd the best cricket of the match.

The West Indies innings was finished off for an addition of nine runs yesterday morning, the one thing that stands out in the memory being a magnificent catch by Hodgson who ran ten yards with his back to a skied ball, turned round, and held it as it swerved away from him. The wisdom of the Lancashire tactics is not always apparent to the uninstructed eye, and it is indeed difficult to understand why Hallows and Watson, who, presumably, knew of L. Green's determination to declare at about 3 o'clock, did not score more than 87 runs in the hour and 20 minutes before luncheon.

During this period Watson scored more than twice as fast as Hallows, a fact hardly as much to the credit of Watson as it is an indictment of Hallows. After luncheon Hallows, by making some beautiful straight drives, a stroke he can make as well as anyone in the country, provided even more damning evidence against his usual methods, and with E. Tyldesley playing like a great batsman in form, the score was raised to 144 by five minutes to 3 o'clock, when Green declared.

This left the West Indies 272 to win with, at the most, just under three hours left for play. Roach and Martin got a good start on the clock by scoring 35 runs together in 20 minutes. Roach, a man who betrays by his very stance at the wicket his intense eagerness to get runs quickly, treated Macdonald and Hodgson as though they were club bowlers. He is exceptionally quick on his feet, and two successive balls of Hodgson's that pitched short outside the offstump were hooked round wide of square leg's left hand. When Iddon and Tyldesley (R.) went on for Macdonald and Hodgson, the story of Monday was repeated, with one important variation. On Monday runs had ceased to come and wickets had fallen, but yesterday, while the runs ceased to come, wickets did not fall. Roach and Martin, who, next to Challenor, understand English wickets better than anyone else on the side, watched the ball far more carefully, and did not show the same unsophisticated belief that the ball advertised in the air its exact intentions off the pitch.

After tea, Roach and Martin went on to play really beautiful cricket. Watching them it was impossible to understand how it was that the team collapsed in the first innings. Roach played as though he saw a potential boundary in every ball, but he is an intelligent enough player to discard his vision the second he sees it is impracticable. He hit three 4's in one over off Hodgson, one lucky one through the slips, and two round to mid-wicket, strokes only made possible by perfect footwork. He was out at 135, caught in two minds by a well pitched-up ball of R. Tyldesley's. L.N. Constantine was leg-before-wicket four runs later. With him disappeared all hopes of a thrilling finish, and all one had left to applaud was an admirable 50 of Martin's.

–The Times,
Wednesday, July 4, 1928, Page 8

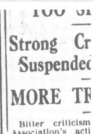

—The Sporting Chronicle, Wednesday, July 4, 1928, Page 6

5.

The 1928 Test Tour

The invitation extended to the WICBC by the MCC for a tour to England in the summer of 1928 had come as no surprise. The argument for a long period of apprenticeship, considered by some elements within the West Indies cricket fraternity as harsh and punitive, could no longer be sustained. The West Indian cricketers had won the day, on the field at home and in England. Their time had come, and only persons with prejudicial attitudes, formed and shaped by circumstances beyond the boundary, were not in agreement.

The WICBC accepted the invitation to tour England, but gave no guarantees of a financial nature about the outcome of the undertaking. They would pay their own way to England, leaving all domestic arrangements to the MCC, who would cover the cost from gate receipts and other income.

Sixteen members of the West Indies team arrived in England at Avonmouth on April 16, and were met in London by Mr. R.H. Mallett, representing the MCC, and the Mayor of London, The Hon. L.H. Tennyson.

On arrival at Paddington Station, London, the West Indians were greeted by weather described as "dismal in the extreme, there being a bitterly cold, driving rain". [*The Times*, April 17, 1928.]

The team consisted of R.K. Nunes (Captain, Jamaica), E.L. Bartlett (Barbados), C.R. Browne (Br. Guiana), G. Challenor (Barbados), L.N. Constantine (Trinidad), M.P. Fernandes (Br. Guiana), G. Francis (Barbados), H.C. Griffith (Barbados), E.L.G. Hoad (Barbados), F.R. Martin (Jamaica), J. Neblett (Br. Guiana), E.A. Rae (Jamaica), C. Roach (Trinidad), W. St. Hill

THE 1928 ARCHIVES

Yorkshire v West Indies
Headingley, Leeds - 4, 5, 6 July, 1928 (3-day match)

Result: Yorkshire won by 190 runs
Umpires: LC Braund and JW Day

Yorkshire 1st innings
P Holmes		b Francis	0
H Sutcliffe		b Griffith	98
A Mitchell	c Fernandes	b Griffith	22
M Leyland	c Small	b Martin	0
W Barber		b Constantine	98
E Robinson	lbw	b Francis	23
C Turner		b Francis	9
*W Rhodes	c Fernandes	b Francis	5
+A Wood		b Constantine	14
GG Macaulay		b Constantine	0
F Dennis	not out		0
Extras	(b 2, b 6, w 4, nb 3)		15
Total	**(all out, 95.4 overs)**		**284**

Francis 22-4-65-4   Griffith 18-4-45-2   Small 16-0-47-0
Martin 20-5-45-1   Hoad 3-0-13-0   Constantine 16.4-3-54-3

West Indies 1st innings
CA Roach	c Macaulay	b Robinson	24
FR Martin	lbw	b Leyland	60
MP Fernandes	lbw	b Rhodes	21
G Challenor	c Robinson	b Rhodes	0
WH St Hill	c Robinson	b Turner	0
ELG Hoad	c Turner	b Rhodes	0
LN Constantine	st Wood	b Rhodes	69
JA Small	c Robinson	b Macaulay	5
*+RK Nunes		b Leyland	16
HC Griffith	c Turner	b Leyland	9
GN Francis	not out		0
Extras	(b 1, lb 3)		4
Total	**(all out, 85.2 overs)**		**208**

Robinson 15-5-24-1   Dennis 10-1-17-0   Macaulay 19-6-33-1
Rhodes 17-7-37-4   Leyland 11.2-2-35-3 Turner 13-3-58-1

Yorkshire 2nd innings
P Holmes	not out		84
H Sutcliffe		b Constantine	27
A Mitchell	not out		51
Extras	(b 1, lb 4, nb 5)		10
Total	**(1 wicket declared, 51 overs)**		**172**

DNB: M Leyland, W Barber, E Robinson, C Turner, *W Rhodes, +A Wood, GG Macaulay, F Dennis.

Francis 13-0-58-0   Griffith 7-1-24-0   Small 3-0-6-0
Constantine 14-5-35-1   Martin 11-2-27-0   Roach 3-0-12-0

West Indies 2nd innings (target: 249 runs)
CA Roach	c Sutcliffe	b Robinson	12
FR Martin	run out		5
MP Fernandes	c Macaulay	b Robinson	2
G Challenor	c Sutcliffe	b Robinson	5
WH St Hill lbw		b Macaulay	1
ELG Hoad	lbw	b Macaulay	15
LN Constantine		b Macaulay	0
JA Small	c Dennis	b Macaulay	3
*+RK Nunes	c Wood	b Macaulay	4
HC Griffith		b Macaulay	0
GN Francis	not out		9
Extras	(b 1, lb 1)		2
Total	**(all out, 38.4 overs)**		**58**

Robinson 19-7-26-3   Macaulay 19.4-6-30-6

MATCH NO. 14
West Indies in England, 1928

The West Indies Test team to England, 1928. Standing from left: J. Scheult (assistant manager), W.H. St. Hill, E.A. Rae, E.L.G. Hoad, J.A. Small, F.R. Martin, L.N. Constantine, H.C. Griffith, O.C. Scott. Seated: E.L. Bartlett, M.P. Fernandes, C.V. Wight (vice-captain), R.K. Nunes (captain), G. Challenor and C.R. Browne. Missing: G.N. Francis, C.A. Powell, and J.M. Neblett.

(Trinidad), O.C. Scott (Jamaica), J.A. Small (Trinidad) and C.V. Wight (Vice-Captain, Br. Guiana). E.A. Rae and J.E. Scheult, the Assistant Manager, travelled via New York. Rae's arrival completed the 17-member touring party.

The selection of the team was made by L.T. Yearwood (Barbados), J.G. Kelshall (Trinidad), C. Shankland (Br. Guiana) and Major G.S. Cox (Jamaica), with H.B.G. Austin, President of the WICBC, in the chair.

The colours adopted for the touring party would be: "deep burgundy blazer with West Indian crest on breast pocket, with tie, sash, &c., of same colour background with a quarter inch stripes of green and silver".

Captain Nunes, speaking to the press at Paddington Station, stated that they were "delighted" that they had been "accorded Test Match rank", and indicated that he had "high hopes for his side". The team, he said was "an extremely well-balanced one in every respect, being even stronger than that of 1923, the batting being stronger, and there being a greater variety of bowling and much better fielding". [*The Times,* April 17, 1928.]

The Captain pointed out that he now had three faster bowlers in his squad. For him, George Francis was as "accurate and fast as he was in 1923", while Learie Constantine "was now faster than either Francis or Griffith".

WEST INDIES AT LEEDS
A DISAPPOINTING PERFORMANCE

At the end of a day's cricket at Leeds, that was watched in pleasantly warm weather by a large crowd, the West Indies scored 22 for no wicket in reply to the Yorkshire total of 284. Two hundred and eighty-four is not a phenomenally large score, but there were times in the day's play when the West Indies, who play the game very strenuously, looked as though they had had too much cricket lately.

When Nunes, who must have forgotten what it is to win it, lost the toss again yesterday, one expected Yorkshire, on a perfect Headingley wicket, to score at least a hundred by luncheon. As it was they lost Holmes, Mitchell, and Leyland for 79 runs. The wicket was too easy for the West Indies fast bowlers, but, for all that, G. Francis bowled Holmes with the third ball of the match, a very good one that swung and broke into him. There would have been some excuse for Mitchell taking half an hour to score a run had he been playing for his place in the eleven, but as a regular member of the Yorkshire team one expects more from him than an instinctive movement back on to the stumps, a turn of the body, and a stroke that sends the ball trickling to mid-on. There is plenty of cricket in Mitchell, but he must be careful to develop and not to stifle it. At 67 M.P. Fernandes, who was keeping wicket, made a clever catch on the leg-side to get rid of him, and two runs later Leyland placed a turning ball of F.R. Martin's into J.A. Small's hands at first slip.

Afterwards Sutcliffe went on to play the cricket of an England batsman. He reached his 50 by hitting a half-volley of L.N. Constantine's past cover-point and in this same over a short ball that leaped up at his head was sent round to the boundary at the fine-leg. He made two beautiful strokes through the slips of Constantine and the other off Francis, but just when he seemed certain to reach his 100 he played back at, and outside, a break-back of Griffith's and his pads which before had religiously "covered up," were not in position to save his off-stump. Barber had in the meantime been playing sound, if unobtrusive, cricket.

During the afternoon the West Indies bowling and fielding fell below the standard those who have watched them consistently have learned to expect. Griffith and Francis stuck to their work splendidly, but Small seems temporarily to have lost his bowling. He was terribly short yesterday and his bowling arm is much lower than it ought to be. Robinson was quickly out after tea, but Wood then came in to make what must have been one of the most amazing strokes the Headingley ground has ever seen. After turning a yorker of Constantine's to the sight-screen he got under the next ball, a short one, and hit over point's head for 6. At 273 he played outside Constantine and was bowled while the next ball which also came back bowled Macaulay. Constantine did not do the "hat-trick," but he finished off the innings with the total at 284. Barber attempted to turn to fine-leg a good-length ball that pitched on his off-stump and hit his leg. Barber was missed at square-leg in the fifties, but, to make up for his disappointment at missing his first 100 by two runs, he has the considerable consolation of knowing that he played an innings which should do much to help him to secure his regular place in the side.

–The Times,
Thursday, July 5, 1928, Page 8

THE WEST INDIES AT LEEDS

CONSTANTINE HITS OUT

Rain and bad light cut short the match between the West Indies and Yorkshire at Leeds yesterday, but nearly four hours' cricket was possible. The West Indies failed by 76 runs to equal Yorkshire's first innings total of 284, although L.N. Constantine, going in at the fall of the fifth wicket, actually scored 69 runs in under 35 minutes.

–The Times,
Friday, July 6, 1928, Page 7

A NATION IMAGINED

The British public had seen Francis, but could hardly believe the rumours that Constantine had developed greater speed than the kind George John had generated on the 1923 tour.

There was considerable excitement among cricket lovers about the West Indies tour. The occasional brilliance of the performances of 1923 had shown that West Indian cricketers were bringing new and spectacular approaches to the various departments of the game. *The Times* reported a view, widely held in the country, that West Indian cricketers were great entertainers who served to alleviate much of the boredom associated with the normal county fare.

Learie Constantine, first West Indian cricket superstar.

Second Class Still

But there remained considerable doubt about the West Indies men as Test players. While it was true, reported *The Times,* that "no touring party has returned [from the West Indies] with an unbeaten record", and that "in their own climate the West Indian cricketers have had the better of their guests", it remained true that "at the moment there is no reason to expect that before Mr. Nunes and his party embark on their return journey they will have proved themselves worthy to join the Australians and the South Africans in Class I, Division I". It was widely believed that while the West Indians had arrived at the Test gate, they were still second-class players with a considerable journey ahead of

THE 1928 ARCHIVES

Nottinghamshire v West Indies
Trent Bridge, Nottingham - 7, 9, 10 July, 1928 (3-day match)

Result: Match drawn
Umpires: WR Cuttell and J Stone

Nottinghamshire 1st innings
G Gunn	c Fernandes	b Francis	0
WW Whysall		b Griffith	80
W Walker	lbw	b Griffith	39
*AW Carr	c Bartlett	b Constantine	100
+B Lilley	c Fernandes	b Griffith	2
GV Gunn	c Francis	b Constantine	6
A Staples	not out		84
F Barratt	lbw	b Martin	45
H Larwood	c Hoad	b Martin	6
SJ Staples	c Griffith	b Martin	0
TL Richmond		b Constantine	2
Extras	(b 25, lb 2, nb 2)		29
Total	**(all out, 97.2 overs)**		**393**

Francis 20-4-69-1   Griffith 26-3-91-3   Neblett 13-2-36-0
Scott 12-1-69-0   Martin 9-2-42-3   Constantine 17.2-2-57-3

West Indies 1st innings
GN Francis		b SJ Staples	21
OC Scott		b Larwood	0
CA Roach	lbw	b SJ Staples	27
FR Martin	c Carr	b SJ Staples	8
EL Bartlett		b Larwood	109
MP Fernandes	c Lilley	b SJ Staples	24
LN Constantine	c A Staples	b Larwood	20
ELG Hoad	lbw	b Barratt	73
*+RK Nunes	c SJ Staples	b Richmond	62
JM Neblett	c Barratt	b SJ Staples	0
HC Griffith	not out		9
Extras	(b 10, lb 14, w 1)		25
Total	**(all out, 131.4 overs)**		**378**

Larwood 12-1-47-3   Barratt 24.4-3-63-1   SJ Staples 41-10-99-5
Richmond 28-5-80-1   A Staples 26-5-64-0

Nottinghamshire 2nd innings
G Gunn		b Constantine	55
WW Whysall	c Fernandes	b Francis	21
W Walker	lbw	b Constantine	36
GV Gunn		b Scott	10
+B Lilley		b Scott	34
A Staples	c Roach	b Scott	12
F Barratt	not out		55
H Larwood	not out		10
Extras	(b 8, lb 1, nb 4)		13
Total	**(6 wickets declared, 64 overs)**		**246**

DNB: *AW Carr, SJ Staples, TL Richmond.

Francis 11-4-35-1   Griffith 9-3-29-0   Neblett 6-1-21-0
Scott 13-0-66-3   Martin 12-2-45-0   Constantine 13-0-37-2

West Indies 2nd innings (target: 262 runs)
GN Francis	not out		18
LN Constantine	not out		67
Extras			0
Total	**(0 wickets, 8 overs)**		**85**

DNB: OC Scott, CA Roach, FR Martin, EL Bartlett, MP Fernandes, ELG Hoad, *+RK Nunes, JM Neblett, HC Griffith.

Whysall 4-0-44-0   Walker 4-0-41-0

MATCH NO. 15 — West Indies in England, 1928

On his way to a century, Learie Constantine makes a stroke against Essex at Leyton in the three-day match in May 1928.

them. England, Australia and South Africa were assessed as equal to be in Division I, Class I. The West Indian team, reported *The Times,* was placed in "Class I, Division II, of the cricket Tripos." [*The Times,* June 14, 1928.]

In some quarters, the West Indies tour was seen as a warm-up and shape-up for the England team that was scheduled to tour Australia that winter. The English selectors were worried about their prospects there, and were keen to observe the pool of players against the West Indies. It was reported that "the West Indians' sole chance of victory" was based "on the possibility that a pair of bowlers – and for this purpose a pair contains three units – will twice go through the batting strength of England". [*The Times,* June 14, 1928.] This chance was described as "remote" because it required bowlers to achieve "pace through the air and off the pitch", something not yet mastered by the West Indians.

"Very possibly," reported *The Times* [June 14, 1928], "the West Indian fast bowlers will enjoy brief spells of startling success in their first Test match, provided that their slips

WEST INDIES DOING WELL
E. L. BARTLETT'S CENTURY

The West Indies made an excellent reply to Nottinghamshire's total of 393 yesterday, scoring 375 runs for nine wickets by the time stumps were drawn. Play began at 12 o'clock yesterday, and will begin at 12 o' clock again to-day. The King and Queen will visit the ground today at 5.10, and both teams will be presented to them.

The West Indies did not do too well up to luncheon, losing three more wickets for an addition of 98 runs. C.A. Roach looked like getting a good deal more than 27 when he tried to turn a ball of S. Staples's and was l-b-w. G. Francis stopped long enough to prove that he was not ostentatiously out of place as a No. 2 batsman, but F.R. Martin, the most dependable batsman on the side at the moment, was out after scoring eight runs. He tried to drive S. Staples through the covers, but the ball turned away from the bat and A.W. Carr, at second slip, got both hands to a ball that went inconveniently wide of him. After luncheon E.L. Bartlett and M.P. Fernandes brought the score up to 195 together in a little over an hour. Fernandes rendered the best possible service to his side by doing no more than keep the ball out of his wicket and watch his partner score the runs. Bartlett played the innings of a man who knows he is on top of the bowling, and is out to get the last ounce of enjoyment out of the situation.

–*The Times*,
Tuesday, July 10, 1928, Page 7

THE KING AT TRENT BRIDGE
A VISIT TO WEST INDIES MATCH

The match between Nottinghamshire and the West Indies was left drawn at Trent Bridge yesterday. The King and Queen arrived on the ground shortly before half-past 5 and both teams were then presented to the King.

The West Indies failed, after all, to gain the first innings lead, E.L.G. Hoad being l-b-w to Barratt after three runs had been added to the overnight score of 375. During the rest of the day the interest in the game was purely technical, as Nottinghamshire made no real effort to get runs quickly, and so give Larwood a chance of putting the West Indies with their backs against the wall. Going in at 12.15, Nottinghamshire scored 64 for the loss of Whysall's wicket. George Gunn was in the mood in which he delights to experiment with, and not punish, the bowlers. The balls he hit he picked out, not because they were obviously inaccurate, but for reasons known only to his own mind. He reached his 50 by walking out to a short ball of Constantine's and hitting it down past point for a single, but a little later Constantine dismissed both him and Walker in the same over. Young Gunn, like his father, sees fast bowling very quickly, and also, like his father, he plays it with his bat in front of his body, and with both feet pointing down the pitch. He reached double figures and was then bowled.

A. Staples was well caught at long-on, and then Barratt came in to score 55 in half an hour. Barratt looked like a large and genial schoolmaster giving fielding practice to a number of immensely enthusiastic small boys. The catches he sent up, however, were high and vigorous enough to give the aggrieved circle of fieldsmen the chance to complain that they were not fair. He hit four 4's in one over, and this feat, together with three 6's, made up an innings that gave immense pleasure to a very large crowd. When Lilley was bowled at 4.20, A.W. Carr declared the innings closed with the total at 246 for six wickets.

–*The Times*,
Wednesday, July 11, 1928, Page 7

give them the support which they have hitherto lacked. Certainly each of them will endeavour to show his colleagues what fast bowling really is. But it is not to be expected that their physical exertions and zealous enthusiasm will seriously incommode Hobbs, Sutcliffe, and the rest."

The English selectors were urged to identify players to engage the West Indians with "at least one eye on the forthcoming Australian tour". [*The Times,* June 14, 1928.] England's captain, A.P.F. Chapman, supported the value of this approach, while stating that to the home team the value of the West Indian tour "lies in the opportunity the matches have afforded for preparing the players for the Australian Test". [*The Sporting Chronicle,* August 16, 1928.] In his judgement, if England's batsmen could handle the pace of Griffith, Francis and Constantine, they would have no difficulty with the Australians.

It was a long and arduous tour. In general, the weather was not good, and West Indian players had much to complain about on this score. Thirty official matches were organised between May 6 and September 8, including three Tests, which were each three days' long. In addition, eight other matches and 'festival' exhibitions were scheduled, as well as the four one-day practice matches which opened the tour in late April. In all, 42 matches were scheduled, requiring the West Indians to play nearly 100 days of cricket in the 142-day tour.

The first of the four one-day practice matches was played against H.D.G. Leveson-Gower's XI at Pelsham, Rye, on April 26, ten days after their arrival. The West Indians scored 224 for two, and restricted the opposition to 90 for six at the close of play. The following practice games yielded similar results. In the second match, the West Indies scored 219 for two, closing play with Reigate Priory on 90 for six. The third match was against Berkansted Club at Ashridge Park, with the West Indies scoring 174 for seven (declared) and Berkansted, 112 for nine. On May 1, they played Dulwich and at the close of play had reached 155 for four to Dulwich's 186. The team seemed to have no difficulty in overwhelming the opposition in these games, which were organised as confidence boosters and welcoming exercises.

Despite this good start, the West Indies raised many eyebrows when they won the first official game against a "strong Derbyshire eleven on a good wicket". [*The Times,* May 7, 1928.] It was an impressive all-round performance against a

Warwickshire v West Indies
Edgbaston, Birmingham - 14, 16, 17 July, 1928 (3-day match)

Result: Warwickshire won by 7 wickets
Umpires: WR Cuttell and D Denton

West Indies 1st innings
Batsman			Runs
G Challenor	c Croom	b Partridge	22
CA Roach		b Speed	11
MP Fernandes		b Speed	0
FR Martin	run out		16
JA Small		b Speed	19
ELG Hoad	c Santall	b Speed	12
LN Constantine	c Parsons	b Croom	70
CR Browne	c Parsons	b Santall	0
*+RK Nunes		b Partridge	13
OC Scott	not out		32
HC Griffith	c Partridge	b Speed	6
Extras	(b 4, lb 4)		8
Total	**(all out, 49.1 overs)**		**209**

Partridge 20-2-84-2 Speed 13.1-2-39-5 Calthorpe 5-0-32-0
Santall 5-1-27-1 Croom 6-0-19-1

Warwickshire 1st innings
Batsman			Runs
+EJ Smith	c Roach	b Constantine	24
N Kilner	c Hoad	b Small	9
LTA Bates	lbw	b Scott	14
RES Wyatt	c Nunes	b Scott	34
JH Parsons	c Constantine	b Scott	161
AJW Croom		b Griffith	69
FR Santall	not out		27
EH King		b Griffith	3
*FSG Calthorpe		b Constantine	9
NE Partridge	c Roach	b Scott	19
AW Speed		b Constantine	2
Extras	(b 8, lb 3, nb 2)		13
Total	**(all out, 109 overs)**		**384**

Griffith 30-8-88-2 Small 18-2-42-1 Constantine 22-1-82-3
Browne 13-1-43-0 Scott 22-1-104-4 Martin 4-0-12-0

West Indies 2nd innings
Batsman			Runs
G Challenor	lbw	b Speed	81
CA Roach	lbw	b Calthorpe	69
MP Fernandes		b Speed	5
FR Martin	lbw	b Wyatt	17
JA Small	lbw	b Speed	32
ELG Hoad	st Smith	b Santall	23
LN Constantine	c Bates	b Speed	0
CR Browne	not out		50
*+RK Nunes	c Smith	b Santall	1
OC Scott	c&b Croom		15
HC Griffith		b Croom	1
Extras	(b 7, lb 9, w 2, nb 1)		19
Total	**(all out, 108.1 overs)**		**313**

Partridge 26-3-66-0 Speed 20-3-60-4 Calthorpe 15-5-21-1
Santall 11-3-40-2 Croom 23.1-1-77-2 Wyatt 13-6-30-1

Warwickshire 2nd innings (target: 139 runs)
Batsman			Runs
+EJ Smith	lbw	b Small	35
N Kilner		b Griffith	15
LTA Bates	retired hurt		6
RES Wyatt	c Roach	b Scott	21
JH Parsons	not out		40
AJW Croom	not out		21
Extras	(lb 1)		1
Total	**(3 wickets, 23.1 overs)**		**139**

DNB: FR Santall, EH King, *FSG Calthorpe, NE Partridge, AW Speed.

Scott 4-0-23-1 Griffith 6-0-41-1 Small 2-0-7-1
Browne 2.1-0-15-0 Constantine 9-0-52-0

team that had finished fifth in the previous County Championship. Though they did not win the second game against Essex, they managed a draw. But with a first innings lead, Constantine's 130 signalled the intent of the team to achieve high performance levels. It was "a truly great innings", *The Times* reported, one that "captured the imagination" and showed that "Constantine was no mere village-green 'slogger', but a batsman with strokes that should put some of our modern batsmen to shame". [*The Times,* May 12, 1928.]

There was the inevitable speculation that the performance to date had been considerably enhanced by good batting pitches on account of warm weather, a circumstance that was not expected to persist. The drawn third game against Surrey indicated at an early stage what was in store for the West Indies later in the tour. J.B. Hobbs (123) and A. Sandham (108), two of England's favoured opening batsmen, established a partnership of 253 that provoked a reporter to conclude that "once the sting is taken out of their fast bowlers, there is so little left". [*The Times,* May 16, 1928.]

It was the aggressive pace of Constantine, Francis and Griffith, however, that prevented

A. Sandham.

THE 1928 ARCHIVES

THE WEST INDIES AT EDGBASTON
CONSTANTINE'S GREAT HITTING

L.N. Constantine gave another demonstration of his fine hitting powers in the match against Warwickshire at Edgbaston on Saturday, but, taken on the whole, the cricket was rather dull. Batting first upon a pitch that was favourable to run-getting, the West Indies cut such a sorry figure that in rather more than an hour they lost half their wickets for 78 runs, and altogether they were dismissed in two hours and 40 minutes for 209. In reply, Warwickshire scored 187 for four, and so finished 22 runs behind with six wickets to fall.

Of the early batsmen G. Challenor alone faced the bowling with any degree of confidence, and it was not until F.R. Martin was joined by L.N. Constantine at the fall of the fifth wicket that a partial recovery was effected. In 20 minutes the pair added 50 runs, both men making several powerful drives before a splendid return by Bates from cover-point let to Martin being run out. Constantine was eighth to leave at 155, and, hitting N.E. Partridge four times to the boundary in one over, he made his 70 out of 77 in 40 minutes. Scott played capital cricket for 50 minutes, but received poor support. A.W. Speed bowled remarkably well.

Warwickshire lost their opening pair – Kilner and Smith – for 39 runs, and, although Bates took 70 minutes to score 14, Parsons afterwards played really delightful cricket, reaching his 50 in three quarters of an hour and completing his 1,000 runs for the season.

–The Times,
Monday, July 16, 1928, Page 5

WARWICK WIN
WEST INDIES BEATEN BY SEVEN WICKETS
SPORTING AND ENJOYABLE GAME

Warwickshire, after a sporting and enjoyable game, achieved victory over the West Indies touring team at Edgbaston to-day by seven wickets.

The fact that L.N. Constantine would be seen at the wickets was responsible for a fairly good attendance of spectators this morning, but they were denied the pleasure of seeing some sensational cricket from the "West Indian Jessop," for he was caught at cover-point by Bates off the first ball he received from A.W. Speed. The latter, bowling from the pavilion end, where he had proved so successful on Saturday, wrought havoc amongst the ranks of the visitors, who, it will be remembered, had scored 209 overnight for the loss of three wickets.

A single was scored off N.E. Partridge, and then Speed hit J.A. Small's pad with the first ball he sent down and the batsman retired lbw. He had contributed 32 to the total. M.P. Fernandes, who had retired overnight through a strain which revived an old injury, came in to resume his innings, with C.A. Roach to run for him, but was quickly sent back by Speed.

Then came the dramatic dismissal of Constantine. Everyone was hoping that the Moseley amateur would perform the "hat-trick," but C.R. Browne, the new comer, prevented its accomplishment.

E.L.G. Hoad and Browne batted steadily, and there was a double change in the bowling at 241. Calthorpe and Croom coming on. Speed, to-day, had sent down six overs and accrued three wickets for 12 runs. At one period he had taken the three for a single.

With his total at 25, Browne skied a ball from Croom to the on-side, and Speed, running from mid-on towards square leg, tried to make a catch, but although he got his hands to the ball, failed to hold it. There had previously been another change in the attack, Wyatt having relieved Calthorpe at 236, and Browne scored two nice 4's – an off-drive and leg hit.

–The Birmingham Mail,
Tuesday, July 17, 1928, Page 5

THE BIRMINGHAM MAIL, SATURDAY, JULY 14, 1928.

TON TENNIS.	CONSTANTINE DELIGHTS CROWD	KENT RETRIEVE
TS H. K. LESTER IN INGLES FINAL.	SPECTACULAR DISPLAY OF HITTING AT EDGBASTON.	AMES SCORES CEN SURRE
S HANDICAP DEFEAT.	70 OUT OF 77.	BIG CROWD AT I Favoured by glorious wea

Surrey from pressing home an advantage.

The inability of the West Indies to defeat Oxford University where they led the first innings by 60 runs, was further evidence, the press reports indicated, that the "bowling, although steady, does not look capable of 'going through' a side". [*The Times*, May 19, 1928.] Despite an impressive century from Small, the batsmen's failure to adjust to the conditions surrounded their performances.

Against Northumberland, Challenor struck a magnificent 146 on a wet, bouncy pitch on which Griffith took 10 wickets in the match, but the media remained convinced that West Indian batsmen seemed impatient and unwilling to adjust to the unfamiliar conditions.

According to one report on the match against Oxford University:

> "The West Indies batsmen have many qualities in common, one of them being the quick, decisive way they get to the over-pitched ball, and another is their failure to get across to the ball outside the off-stump pitched a foot short of orthodox good length. A stroke that can be played safely on their own perfect pitches is dangerous here and, unless they give up what is really a firm-footed slash at the ball, they will lose many wickets." [*The Times*, May 19, 1928.]

Comments such as these on the technical deficiencies of West Indies batsmen were commonplace during the drawn match against the MCC (May 19-22), and the win against Cambridge University (May 26-28). By the end of May, however, the West Indians were not performing badly. They had suffered no defeats, and had three victories to feel proud about. Batsmen were scoring centuries and bowlers were getting wickets.

June, however, saw a sudden turn of events. The West Indies visited Ireland, and took on an XI that had no reason to consider itself a match for the West Indies. June 4-6 were the dates of the Irish disaster, the shattering defeat of the touring side by a team of 'irregulars'.

Returning to England after what was described as the 'Dublin fiasco', West Indies batsmen especially were mauled by public opinion as the first Test approached. Constantine saved the day for the West Indies in the next game against Middlesex with a brilliant all-round performance that won the game, but masked the weakness of the top order. Perceived to be less accurate than Francis, Constantine bowled the "faster and more dangerous ball". *The Times*, describing the West Indies victory as 'Constantine's

THE 1928 ARCHIVES

Worcestershire v West Indies
County Ground, New Road, Worcester - 18, 19 July, 1928 (2-day match)

Result: Match drawn
Umpires: W Phillips and AE Street

West Indies 1st innings

CA Roach	lbw	b Gilbert	38
FR Martin	c Summers	b Tarbox	77
ELG Hoad	not out		149
*+RK Nunes	lbw	b Root	38
CR Browne	c King	b Root	0
WH St Hill	c&b	Gilbert	16
OC Scott	st Summers	b Gibbons	75
CV Wight	not out		1
Extras	(b 9, lb 6, w 1)		16
Total	**(6 wickets declared, 139 overs)**		**410**

DNB: EA Rae, GN Francis, HC Griffith.

Root 38-14-80-2   Tarbox 43-10-149-1   Gilbert 42-9-109-2
Nichol 4-0-27-0   Gibbons 7-0-20-1   Wright 5-2-9-0

Worcestershire 1st innings

HHI Gibbons	not out		200
L Wright	c&b	Francis	7
M Nichol	c Martin	b Hoad	104
WV Fox	not out		104
Extras	(b 16, lb 2, nb 6)		24
Total	**(2 wickets, 122 overs)**		**439**

DNB: HA Gilbert, CV Tarbox, BW Quaife, CF Walters, JW King, CF Root, +FT Summers.

Francis 23-8-65-1   Griffith 27-4-99-0   Browne 24-8-49-0
Scott 18-1-86-0   Martin 17-5-49-0   Hoad 8-1-46-1
Roach 5-0-21-0

WEST INDIES BAT ALL DAY

Owing to the fact that the second Test Match will be begun at Manchester on Saturday, Worcestershire's game with the West Indies, which was begun yesterday at Worcester, is limited to two days. The West Indies batted first, and at the close of play had scored 410 for six wickets.

C.A. Roach and F.R. Martin laid the foundation of this good total by putting on 73 together for the first wicket, and at luncheon the tourists had 119 runs on the board with only one wicket down. On the game being resumed, runs were hard to get against the bowling of Root and Tarbox, and in an hour the score was increased by no more than 38. The second wicket fell at 165, Martin, who hit eight 4's having batted for three hours and scored 77, while afterwards, both E.L.G. Hoad and R.K. Nunes refused to take the slightest risk, Hoad being at the wicket two hours before reaching 50. With the total up to 238, Root got rid of Nunes, who had made 38 in 55 minutes, and tea was then taken.

After the interval the West Indies for a time fared badly, C.R. Browne being out to the first ball sent down, and W.H. St. Hill falling to a spectacular catch by H.A. Gilbert, who held a very hard return. Hoad, however, reached his 100 after a stay of three hours and 50 minutes – this was his first three-figure innings of the tour – and when joined by Scott runs came at a great pace, 148 being added in 90 minutes.

–The Times, Thursday, July 19, 1928, Page 7

MATCH NO. 17

West Indies in England, 1928

Constantine at Middlesex, 1928.

Triumph', gave an account of his performance that set him apart as perhaps the first superstar of West Indies cricket with no equal on the world stage:

"Constantine's fielding on the first day, his batting yesterday definitely established his claim to be considered as the most determined match-winning cricketer in the world. It is seldom that the Pavilion at Lord's twice rises to a player in one day; but yesterday Constantine was accorded the honour – and it is a very considerable one – first, before luncheon, when he ratted out the Middlesex batsmen, and towards the end of the match, when he had won the match for his side by a gloriously daring display of batsmanship. ... Such compliment as he was paid by every one at Lord's yesterday, spectators, card-sellers, groundsmen, gatemen and all the others who should have been attending to their particular business, probably not even excluding the umpires and the scorers, and most certainly including the beaten side, was remarkable, but no more than he deserved." [*The Times,* June 13, 1928.]

Two days earlier Constantine had been described as arguably the best all-round cricketer on English soil.

Whatever the level of encouragement within the West Indies camp as a result of the win over Middlesex was removed the following week when the Minor Counties, probably one of the weakest teams on the first-class circuit, handed the tourists their first defeat in England. Images of the 'Dublin fiasco' were revived as the West Indies tumbled at Exeter to defeat by 42 runs. Granted, the West Indies had

THE 1928 ARCHIVES

Second Test - England v West Indies

Old Trafford, Manchester, England - 21, 23, 24 July, 1928
England won by an innings & 30 runs

West Indies 1st innings

G Challenor	run out		24
CA Roach	lbw	b AP Freeman	50
FR Martin	run out		21
WH St Hill	c VWC Jupp	b MW Tate	3
ELG Hoad	lbw	b VWC Jupp	13
*+RK Nunes		b AP Freeman	17
LN Constantine	lbw	b VWC Jupp	4
CR Browne	c JC White	b AP Freeman	23
OC Scott	c APF Chapman	b AP Freeman	32
GN Francis		b AP Freeman	1
HC Griffith	not out		1
Sundries	BY: 10 LB: 7 NB: 0 WD: 0 PN: 0		17
Total	**RR: 1.95 runs/6 balls**		**206**

FoW: 1-48, 2-100, 3-105, 4-113, 5-129, 6-133, 7-158, 8-185, 9-203, 10-206

MW Tate 35-13-68-1   WR Hammond 6-2-16-0   AP Freeman 33.4-18-54-5
VWC Jupp 18-5-39-2   JC White 13-6-12-0

England 1st innings

JB Hobbs	c WH St Hill	b CR Browne	53
H Sutcliffe	c RK Nunes	b HC Griffith	54
GE Tyldesley		b CR Browne	3
WR Hammond	c CA Roach	b LN Constantine	63
DR Jardine	run out		83
*APF Chapman	retired hurt		3
MW Tate		b HC Griffith	28
VWC Jupp	c LN Constantine	b HC Griffith	12
JC White	not out		21
+H Elliott	lbw	b OC Scott	6
AP Freeman	lbw	b OC Scott	0
Sundries	BY: 15 LB: 3 NB: 6 WD: 1 PN: 0		25
Total	**RR: 3.27 runs/6 balls**		**351**

FoW: 1-119, 2-124, 3-131, 4-251, 5-285, 6-311, 7-326, 8-351, 9-351

GN Francis 23-4-68-0   OC Scott 9.2-0-28-2   LN Constantine 25-7-89-1
HC Griffith 25-7-69-3   CR Browne 25-2-72-2

West Indies 2nd innings

G Challenor	c H Elliott	b WR Hammond	0
CA Roach	c DR Jardine	b MW Tate	0
FR Martin	c WR Hammond	b AP Freeman	32
WH St Hill	c WR Hammond	b JC White	38
ELG Hoad	lbw	b AP Freeman	4
GN Francis	c MW Tate	b AP Freeman	0
*+RK Nunes	c substitute	b AP Freeman	11
LN Constantine	c H Sutcliffe	b AP Freeman	18
CR Browne	c H Elliott	b JC White	7
OC Scott	not out		3
HC Griffith	c WR Hammond	b JC White	0
Sundries	BY: 1 LB: 1 NB: 0 WD: 0 PN: 0		2
Total	**RR: 2.42 runs/6 balls**		**115**

FoW: 1-0, 2-2, 3-57, 4-67, 5-71, 6-79, 7-93, 8-108, 9-115, 10-115

MW Tate 9-4-10-1   WR Hammond 6-0-23-1   AP Freeman 18-5-39-5
C White 14.3-4-41-3

MATCH NO. 18
West Indies in England, 1928

the worst of the bad weather, but the focus and concentration of the home team served to illustrate deficiencies in the West Indies batting on the eve of the first Test, which pleased the MCC officials who had turned out in large numbers to witness the spectacle.

Constantine gears up.

West Indies fielding against Derby during the 1928 tour, Smith is batting.

SECOND TEST MATCH
WEST INDIES FALL AWAY AFTER GOOD START
SOUND EFFORT BY C.A. ROACH

The second Test match between England and the West Indies was commenced at Old Trafford to-day. The West Indies, who won the toss and took first innings, made a good start, though their batting at times was extremely restrained, and at lunch the score stood at 94 for one.

A startling change came over the game following the resumption of play, five wickets falling for the addition of 37 runs.

While cloudy and appreciably cooler than for some little time past, the weather was quite fine and pleasant, but the company present at the start in no way suggested a Test game. Indeed, at half-past eleven, when the match began, the attendance probably numbering under 3,000, would have been poor for an ordinary county fixture. Still, following the recent spell of dry weather, the ground was in excellent order, and Nunes, beating Chapman in the toss, had no hesitation in deciding to bat.

...Punctually to time, the England eleven turned into the field, Roach and Challenor opened the West Indies batting against Tate and Hammond, Roach scored three off each bowler, but the first of these strokes might have led to a run-out had Hobbs, at cover, possessed his old dash. Curiously enough, after three overs, sawdust was called for, but the reason for the demand was not apparent. The total had only reached 10 when, in Hammond's second over, Challenor, with his score at 2, was badly missed at slip by Chapman, who seemed rather taken by surprise. Following upon this blunder runs came freely, six overs producing 26.

HOBBS' SMART RETURN

The weather towards noon turned very gloomy, but the attendance had increased to about 7,000. Play became quieter, and, while Roach batted soundly, Challenor was beaten by Tate and nearly caught off that bowler. Freeman relieved Hammond at 31 and began with four maidens, while in his fifth over Challenor nearly played on. Meanwhile Jupp had displaced Tate, the batting being so weak after the first few overs that no more than 13 runs were added in forty minutes, seven of these moreover, being extras. The pitch badly lacked life.

To defence so exclusively did Roach devote himself that his score remained at 14 for three-quarters of an hour. Challenor was given 4 runs by a piece of misfielding, and Elliott missed stumping him off Freeman when 23; but at 48 the batsmen were separated, a sharp single being attempted and a smart return by Hobbs to the wicket-keeper resulting in Challenor being run out after a stay of sixty-five minutes. Martin, who followed, shaped well, but there was no real departure from the cautious game which the tourists had set themselves to play until the match had lasted ninety minutes.

Roach then surprised the crowd by hitting the two following balls from Freeman for 4, bringing on White for Freeman at 72, while when Tate resumed, he treated that bowler similarly, but these were the only strokes of note during the long spell. Lunch time arrived with the total at 94 for one wicket, a very satisfactory morning's work for the Tourists.

BIG ATTENDANCE

The weather continued cloudy, but so many people arrived during the luncheon interval that on resuming the attendance amounted to fully 12,000. Not until twenty minutes past two did the West Indies resume their innings. Tate shared the attack with Freeman and beat each batsman in turn, but Roach, wanting only one for his 50 at the adjournment, only reached that number after he had played five minutes of sound workmanlike batting.

The 100 was reached in two hours and ten minutes, but before another run had been added Roach's excellent innings which included five 4's, came to an end on an appeal for leg-before. The partnership for the second wicket extended over seventy minutes, and produced 52 runs. St. Hill, who followed, was easily caught at short leg at 103. Hoad then joined Martin, who lost his wicket curiously. Martin played a ball which, hitting White at mid-off, rose high off that fieldsman's foot. Martin went for a run which Hoad would not have, and Freeman, gathering the ball, returned it to the wicketkeeper, who ran Martin out.

Martin when dismissed in dubious fashion had batted 90 minutes for 21, three wickets having fallen in 40 minutes since lunch for the addition of 19 runs. Hoad and Nunes naturally exercised much care. They shaped well, although runs came very slowly, and White and Jupp took up the attack. Half an hour's play after the fall of the fourth wicket yielded only 13 runs...

CONSTANTINE FAILS

Hoad and Nunes took forty minutes to add 16. The crowd endured the dull cricket most patiently. Hoad was leg-before at 129. Constantine, who followed, was loudly cheered, and the fieldsmen spread out, but the newcomer to the third ball he received was also leg before, the West Indies, despite their cautious methods, having six men out for 133.

Browne joined Nunes, who batted an hour for 7. The official returns gave the number paying for admission up to four o'clock as 10,226.

—The Birmingham Mail,
Saturday, July 21, 1928, Page 5

6.

Winning Battles in a Losing War

First Test

Inevitably, Lord's was the venue of the historic encounter between West Indies and England. The game started at 11:30 a.m. on Saturday, June 23. The great Jack Hobbs was not available, but the England team was made up of the "best cricketers" in the country. The West Indies team was not expected to win, but no one doubted its ability to "ensure a large attendance and a keen game." [*The Times,* June 23, 1928.]

The English selectors gave no surprises when they announced the following team:

A.P.F. Chapman – Captain (Kent)	V.W.C. Jupp (Northamptonshire)
D.R. Jardine (Surrey)	H. Sutcliffe (Yorkshire)
C. Hallows (Lancashire)	W.R. Hammond (Gloucestershire)
E. Tyldesley (Lancashire)	M.W. Tate (Sussex)
H. Larwood (Nottinghamshire)	H. Smith (Gloucestershire)
A.P. Freeman (Kent)	M. Leyland – 12th man (Yorkshire)

This was a well-balanced and powerful team. Hammond and Sutcliffe were batsmen of the highest class, and Freeman, Larwood and Tate were rated as the best bowling attack of the time. Ernest Tyldesley, however, was the man to watch. He had been a member of Lord Tennyson's XI that had visited the West Indies in 1926. His two centuries in the early part of the tour had set him apart as a class player for West Indian spectators.

The Hobbs-Sutcliffe opening partnership was established

SLOW, BUT NOT SURE

West Indies Out for 206 Despite Cautious Batting

The close of play in the second Test match, which commenced at Old Trafford, Manchester, yesterday, found England in a strong position against the West Indies. The visitors were dismissed for the very modest total of 206, to which England responded with 84 without loss. Thus, with all their wickets intact, England are only 122 behind.

The tourists gave a very moderate batting display, particularly after the fall of the second wicket at 100. The first wicket put on 48, and the second contributed 32, but thereafter the best stand was that for the eighth wicket, and that produced only 27 runs.

C.A. Roach alone showed any mastery over the varied England bowling, but after scoring 30 out of 98 he was dismissed l.b.w.

The tourists were cautious to an extreme. The batsmen watched the ball right up to the bat, and few of the players indulged in hitting, except in the event of an occasional loose ball being sent down. The running was not good, and both Challenor and Martin were the victims of "run out" decisions.

So cautious was the batting throughout that long intervals went without a run being scored. R.K. Nunes, for instance, scored 3 in an hour and, in all, got 17 out of 72 in 90 minutes.

Freeman was the most successful bowler, and took half of the wickets at a cost of slightly under 11 runs apiece. His last spell was particularly deadly, for in two balls less than the dozen overs, he bowled six maiden overs, took four of his wickets and conceded only 22 runs.

Tate bowled well, but he was not suited by the pitch, and his one wicket proved rather expensive. He did some useful work, however, and was responsible for the running out of Challenor when the first wicket looked like proving difficult to capture, Roach played a ball hard towards mid-off, and a run looked quite safe, but Tate returned the ball so promptly and accurately that the wicket-keeper was able to break the wicket before Challenor could get home. Tate also had a hand in the running out of Martin, taking a hot return from Freeman.

Hobbs and Sutcliffe opened England's reply to the bowling of Constantine and Francis, and, for a long time, found run-getting a matter of considerable difficulty consequent upon accurate bowling and brilliant fielding.

Sutcliffe was particularly slow in getting going, but, subsequently, he scored at a faster pace than his partner. When stumps were drawn the Yorkshireman was 39 and Hobbs 32, extras accounting for 13.

Late in the day Griffith had the galling experience of being no-balled on four out of five successive deliveries.

–The Sunday Mercury, Sunday, July 22, 1928, Front Page

PITCH AND PAVILION
Inside Information About the Leading County Clubs

WARWICKSHIRE

The West Indies provided a real treat at Edgbaston last week-end, and the cricket was the most interesting seen at the venue for some time. Not only so but the "gates" were exceptionally good and the total receipts of over £1,000 – from which, of course, the West Indies take a share – will gladden the heart of the Warwickshire treasurer.

"Jack" Parson's name has been much in the news this past week. There was his remarkable if not unique feat of hitting four 6's off four successive balls from O.C. Scott, the tourists' slow right arm bowler, on Monday, and a day or two afterwards came the announcement that at the end of this season he is to sever his professional connection with Warwickshire and will in the near future be ordained in the Church of England.

Parson's career as a regular member of the Warwickshire eleven started in 1911 – their championship year – when his batting average for 16 matches was 23.91.

For a time after the war he stayed in the Army, but he resumed his cricketing career with Warwickshire in 1923 and has done consistently well since, scoring his thousand runs regularly every season.

–The Sunday Mercury, Sunday, July 22, 1928, Page 12

as England's premier pair since 1924. It was a crucial part of the 3-0 victory at home over the South Africans. In this five-match series, they plundered the South African bowling and emerged in some ratings as the best opening partnership in English Test cricket history.

In the first Test at Edgbaston, Hobbs made a patient 76 and Sutcliffe, a more commanding 64. By the second Test at Lord's, however, they had seen enough of the South African bowling and began the process of tearing it apart. Hobbs' 211 and Sutcliffe's 122 saw England to 268 before the first wicket fell. The West Indies, then, comforted by the knowledge that Hobbs was unavailable for the first Test, had to contend only with the power and supreme confidence of Sutcliffe, who was expected to open the batting with C. Hallows, the Lancashire number one.

Not yet a legend, Walter Wally Hammond came in at number four.

Ernest Tyldesley's position at number three was expected. He had made his Test debut against Australia in 1921, but did not show his class until the 1927 tour to South Africa, when he topped the batting averages with 520 runs at 65. As the first Test against the West Indies approached, he was in splendid form at Lancashire. He maintained a high level of performance during that summer, amassing a staggering 3,024 runs at an average of 79.

Batting at number four was Walter (Wally) Hammond, who was already preparing to project his legendary reputation as one of the greatest batsmen of all time. He was known for the grace and elegance of his stroke play, and

FEEBLE BATS
TOURISTS FLATTER OUR BOWLING

When England won the first Test match against the West Indies an undeserved viture was read into England's attack.

I fear there will be the same satisfaction taken from the cheap dismissal of the West Indies at Old Trafford on Saturday in the second of the series of three.

Actually the Indians should have taken 400 runs out of a wicket of uniform and even pace, the best for batting that any ground can provide, and against so much innocuous bowling bestowed upon them.

Sheer enfeebled batsmanship is the only description possible for a mere total of 206.

Much sympathy as we feel for the visitors, no first-class side should be the victims of methods so elementary. It comes to this again; they are confounded by slow bowling with the less spin than flight, and they are temperamental to a serious fault of misjudgment.

Then, one finds two wickets thrown away by bad mistakes in running and three object cases of leg-before-wicket, including Constantine, whose effervescence was contributory to his own downfall.

This was one of the tragedies for the crowd of 15,000, the numbers paying being round 10,500, who were subject to an ordeal of slow batting quite opposed to the character and attributes of the West Indies style.

When they did go out to the slow ball it was with an almost boyish abandon, and Elliott, the Derbyshire wicketkeeper, playing in his first Test in this country, did not distinguish himself by missing two gift chances of stumping.

All these things considered, then, England's bowling is entirely falsely represented in the West Indies small total. Taken through the Australian perspective we are to toil for days out there if unable to produce something better.

V.W.C. Jupp, flattered at Lord's, was no less so on this occasion. He could not turn the ball, and with his flighting should have been hit for a quantity of 4's.

C.R. Browne in scoring 23 out of 25 in 20 minutes for the seventh wicket showed how to do it.

The rest were timorous in playing back and trying to cover up with their pads. Two backed up too far, and allowed Freeman to bowl them round their legs.

Although taking five wickets for 54, and going on for the last time four of them for 22, Freeman could be short and pitch half-volleys on the leg side with impunity.

Such bowling as we saw on Saturday, the first pair of Australian batsmen would probably have played all day.

–The Sporting Chronicle,
Monday, July 23, 1928, Front Page

THE SECOND TEST MATCH
THE WEST INDIES

In the first Test Match at Lord's the West Indies gave the impression that their batting strength is not sufficient to give them any real chance of beating England under equal conditions. The deficit is of temperament rather than of technique, and will be less apparent as their experience grows. But at present their batsmen, with the exception of G. Challenor and R.K. Nunes, are easily lured on big occasions into adopting tactics which the bowlers, particularly the slow bowlers, desire to impose upon them, and their judgment in running is elementary. C.A. Roach is not to be blamed unreservedly for the loss of Challenor's wicket on Saturday. Mortal man could not be expected to guess that Hobb's cricket sense would enable him to stop and return the ball as he did, but the running out of F.R. Martin was clearly due to over-excitement. The English bowlers did all that was necessary by going through the side without charging the Board of Control for more than one new ball on a wicket which was as easy as any groundsman can make it. If they were helped by two run-outs, they were unfortunate at the start, when the ball at short intervals flew up in the slips just out of reach of the fieldsmen, and Elliott was out of form though after the first hour he recovered and kept wicket well, but why he omitted to stump Challenor when he had the ball in his hand and the batsman was a long yard out of his ground is a mystery which he alone can solve.

Tate is, as he very well knows, an unlucky bowler. On Saturday he was constantly missing the stumps or the edge of the bat by the veriest fraction of an inch and a large proportion of the runs scored off him resulted from unintentional snicks. Freeman must have enjoyed himself hugely, and V.W.C. Jupp was made to look abnormally guileful. That the English attack would have sufficed to gain an advantage over an average Australian team is not to be affirmed, shrewdly as A.P.F. Chapman directed it, and the fielding was not much better than the proverbial curate's egg. Chapman, depending as circumstances dictated that he must, on his three slow bowlers, had to post Tate, J.C. White, and Jupp on the boundary at intervals, but, on the day, the deep field was a restful place.

–The Times,
Monday, July 23, 1928, Page 6

was clearly a player in the seemingly effortless mould. Critically, it was understood that the Gloucestershire man had no discernible fear of fast bowling. This was amply demonstrated in the summer of 1927, when he smashed away at Lancashire's fearsome fast-bowling menace, E.A. McDonald, during an innings of 187 at Old Trafford.

Equally significant was his emergence as a class player in the West Indies during the MCC tour of 1926-27. West Indians watched in awe as Wally amassed the extraordinary total of 733 runs at an average of 45.85, including a magnificent 238 at Kensington Oval in Barbados. The Barbadians recognised his special quality, and at the height of Wally's fame, took delight in recalling his early West Indian exploits. In the 1927 county championship, before the wickets hardened in June to welcome the Test series, he had already made 1,000 runs. This was bad news for the West Indians, who knew that an in-form Hammond was a formidable proposition.

If the West Indians were expecting that they could now place a greater degree of confidence in their bowling attack, the English regarded their team as well balanced, if not impressive in all departments. Behind the reputation of a distinguished batting line-up could be found a bowling unit ideally suited to the June conditions. The menacing Larwood and the highly effective Tate would open the bowling, with Freeman and Jupp representing the spin department.

Harold Larwood was only 24 in 1928.

Hammond, too, had done well with the ball as a deceptive seamer, and was expected to complement the pace armoury.

Harold Larwood was a mere 24-year-old, and was the pacer expected to give West Indian openers a hard time with his known and steep bounce from a good length. He was fully enjoying his reputation as England's fastest bowler, and there was no shortage of experts to argue that he was the quickest in the game. The Nottinghamshire hero was a

THE SECOND TEST MATCH

WEST INDIES' BIG TASK

England's batsmen complied quite a respectable score yesterday in the Second Test Match at Manchester, but they had to fight hard for their runs all the time. Unless some new bowlers of pace have recently been discovered in Australia, it is highly improbable that our men during the coming winter will have to face an attack of such sustained ferocity as that provided by Francis, Constantine, and Griffith. Collectively these three may reasonably claim to be considered just about as formidable as were Gregory and Macdonald in 1921. This pair, it must be remembered, were supported by Australian fielding. The West Indies yesterday fielded anything but well.

In the first hour of the day three catches were missed which certainly should have been made. Considering that these chances were offered by Hobbs and Tyldesley, the perpetrators of the mistakes may congratulate themselves that they were not very expensive. But three men – Roach, St. Hill, and Constantine – distinctly achieved merit.

Although they had to put up with so many disappointments, the fast bowlers never became despondent, and their physical stamina was more than equal to the strain imposed on it. Constantine's fastest spell of bowling was his last. All through the piece Francis and Griffith were able to make the ball run away from the off stump. Browne, the slow bowler, kept an admirable length, and made the ball swing in late from the off. His chief business was to keep down runs while the fast bowlers were resting. In the execution of his duty he took the first two wickets that fell. Critics who consider the English batting dull and unenterprising do less than justice to the quality of the West Indies bowling.

A little rain fell in Manchester during Sunday night. It may have taken a trifle of pace out of the wicket, but it did not otherwise affect it seriously. The ball continued to come on stump-high at most, and the eye of faith through which every good bowler sees facts was required to detect an occasional break-back. Hobbs and Sutcliffe continued their partnership with less than normal mastery. Fine strokes there were, of course, but interposed with them were several made in a hurry, and two which should have cut short their endeavour to bring up the hundred. Hobbs, trying to place Constantine round the corner, pushed the ball well within the reach of short leg, but Challenor was slow to move and omitted to make the catch.

At the other end Francis made him edge the going-away ball to first slip, where Browne missed as easy a chance as a man may get in that position off a fast bowler.

HOBBS'S DISMISSAL

Browne then came on for Constantine. Hobbs clearly regarded him as one to be hit into the middle of the ensuing week, but his second attempt to do so sent the ball high into the long field, where St. Hill made a well-judged catch. Tyldesley had barely cracked his duck when he was missed at short mid-on by Francis. The fieldsman was standing preposterously close to the bat, but those who stand there chance that sort of thing. Jardine and Hammond then began their long partnership. It was not remarkably eventful. Hammond was not lifting his bat so high, or so freely, as he normally does. Perhaps in consequence of that, his forcing back-stroke beat the off side field less frequently than usual. Jardine, possibly because the bowlers persistently aimed at his leg stump, concentrated mainly on onside play. On the off-side he cut the shorter balls beautifully, but in driving he did not regularly synchronize footwork with the swing of his bat. The pair were together at luncheon time, when the first innings lead had been secured.

Soon after the interval Hammond was very well caught by Roach, fielding rather close in at cover-point. Roach flung himself full length and just got his fingers under the ball. Chapman almost immediately strained a muscle in his thigh as he finished a sharp run. The accident caused him to retire, and he could not, or, at any rate, did not, resume his innings later. As Jupp was lame, Tate was next man in. He opened quietly, but Jardine now began to score at a great pace. Unfortunately he was run out, an accident for which Tate must take the responsibility. Jardine hit Scott to long-leg, and the stroke was always worth two runs. Tate declined Jardine's call and, when his predominant partner charged down to his end, he lost his head and omitted to take two steps out of his ground and cross him. On a previous occasion he had come near to being out. He played a ball to square-leg and, in starting to run, slipped his foot on to his stumps. The umpire properly ruled him not out. Subsequently Tate made a few powerful hits, especially off Constantine, who bowled viciously fast at him, but the last few wickets fell at decent intervals, and the innings closed at tea-time for 351.

Neither Chapman nor Judd came out to field when the West Indies started their second innings. White took over the captaincy, and Leyland and Taylor acted as substitutes.

–The Times,
Tuesday, July 24, 1928, Page 8

thrill for spectators and a nightmare for batsmen. His perfectly balanced delivery stride at the end of a long, elegant run to the wicket set him apart as an artist who was the model for other fast bowlers. Before he fully distinguished himself as a dangerous and ruthless pacer in the famous 'Body Line' series against the Aussies in 1933, Larwood was feared internationally but admired for the beauty of his action.

Partnering Larwood, was Maurice Tate, the 23-year-old Sussex medium-face pacer. He was considered the ideal support for Larwood because of their contrasting styles and approaches. Unlike Larwood, Tate was a big man with an over-powering frame that gave him a rolling gait. Larwood's 18-yard run to the wicket was an attraction in itself, while Tate rolled in from a mere eight yards, but had the ability to surprise batsmen because of his speed off the wicket. It was the norm to see keepers and slips standing back at the same distance for both bowlers, a circumstance that perplexed and unnerved many batsmen. He was known especially for his devastating, late out-swinger and menacing, sharp, lifting in-cutter. With a reputation as the master of the late-cutting ball, Tate was ample proof that pace was not always the key to wicket taking, but control, swing and late movement.

Alfred P. Freeman, the senior spinner.

Alfred Percy Freeman, known in the cricket world as "Tich", was the senior spinner. A short man, just over five ft., he had established himself as Kent's leading spinner before the First World War. In 1928, he was already 40 years old, but was still able to capture 304 wickets for Kent in that season. His googly and top-spinner were already legendary when the West Indies arrived. But importantly, he was known as a bowler who could hold up an end for hours with accurate, economical wrist-spin.

Hobbs was expected to be available for the second Test. No one expected Hallows to withstand the transition. Hobbs

THE 1928 ARCHIVES

ENGLAND'S EASY WIN

WEST INDIES BEATEN BY AN INNINGS AND 30 RUNS

FREEMAN'S TEN WICKETS

ST. HILL'S PLUCKY INNINGS FOR TOURISTS

The Second Test Match between England and the West Indies came to an early close at Old Trafford, Manchester, to-day.

England won by an innings and 30 runs. So strongly, in the first two stages, had the match between England and the West Indies at Manchester gone in favour of the home country that the public evidently expected an early finish. At 11 o'clock the company present at Old Trafford amounted to only a few hundred.

The position was that West Indies, 145 behind on the first innings, had, at their second attempt, in the course of eighty minutes' cricket last evening, before bad light brought play to a close, lost four batsmen for 71 runs and thus with six wickets to fall required 74 more runs to escape a single innings defeat. The prospects of the tourists, moreover, had not been improved by rain, which, if never heavy, had fallen for some time last night.

This morning the weather was dull and threatening and very much cooler than on either of the previous days.

A.P.F. Chapman, consequent upon his injury yesterday, did not turn out, J.C. White again acting as captain. V.W.C. Jupp, owing to knee trouble, was also an absentee, Leyland and Taylor, of Lancashire, completing the home fielding eleven.

St. Hill (33) and Francis had White and Freeman against them and the fourth ball Freeman sent down Francis skied to Tate at short leg, half the visiting team being thus out for 71.

Joined by Nunes, St. Hill made one fine stroke off White, but at 79 was brilliantly caught at slip by Hammond. Batting in capital form for 85 minutes St. Hill had six 4's, mostly pulls, in his 38. Constantine, who followed, had made only a single when he skied a ball from White to a great height and was missed from an awkward chance by Freeman at mid-off.

Following upon Constantine's escape 10 runs were added, but then Nunes, who had shaped quite well, put the ball up tamely to short leg, and was caught by Taylor. With Browne in, Constantine, in one over from White, scored a 4 and four 2's, the 100 being reached inside two hours.

The next over, however, he lifted a ball from Freeman straight into the hands of Sutcliffe, standing close to the bowling screen, the eighth wicket going down at 108. Seven runs later a catch at the wicket dismissed Browne, and Griffith, off the first ball he received, was brilliantly taken low down at slip by Hammond. Thus at five minutes to twelve West Indies were all out for 115.

The Tourists, who batted altogether two hours and ten minutes, lost six wickets this morning in fifty minutes, for 44 runs. Freeman, in the course of the match, took ten wickets for 93 runs.

England won the first Test match at Lord's by an innings and 58 runs. The third and last Test match commences at the Oval on August 11.

–The Birmingham Mail,
Tuesday, July 24, 1928, Page 5

CHALLENOR just fails to get home in time in the International match at Old Trafford, Manchester.

—*The Sporting Chronicle, Monday, July 23, 1928, Page 6*

and Sutcliffe were believed to exist in the natural order of things, only to be disrupted by death or illness. Many would not have known that Hobbs, the great Surrey player, who was knighted in 1953 for outstanding services to cricket, was born in 1882, which meant that he was at the ripe old age of 46 when he was preparing to take on the West Indies pace attack.

Known throughout England as "The Master", Hobbs was an attacking batsman who spotted line and length very early and always seemed to be in position. He was a keen, if not compulsive hooker, and English fans were excited at the prospects of his combat with a West Indies all-out pace attack. The West Indian bowlers were eager to have an opportunity to engage the old master, who had developed the knack of scoring centuries at will, against the finest and fastest bowlers. His reputation was everywhere and certainly all West Indian players and cricket fans knew of his record of achievement.

Behind him stood the charismatic captain, Arthur Frank Chapman, "Percy" for short, but a giant, standing at 6 ft. 3 ins., with a bouncy mop of curly, blonde hair. He was a Cambridge man, who two years earlier, at the age of 26, had taken England's captaincy from A.W. Carr in the Australian series. From that time, he had been riding a crest as the man expected to restore England's leadership of the

Hobbs (left) and Sutcliffe going out to bat.

THE 1928 ARCHIVES

Wales v West Indies
Llandudno Cricket Club Ground - 25, 26, 27 July, 1928, (3-day match)

Result: Wales won by 8 wickets
Umpires: A Morton and WR Parry

West Indies 1st innings

G Challenor	lbw	b Barnes	50
CA Roach	c Ryan	b Barnes	4
WH St Hill	lbw	b Barnes	20
*+RK Nunes		b Ryan	25
OC Scott		b Barnes	7
CR Browne		b Barnes	0
LN Constantine	c Barnes	b Ryan	24
EA Rae	c Ryan	b Barnes	0
JM Neblett		b Barnes	17
CV Wight	not out		16
GN Francis		b Ryan	3
Extras	(b 21, lb 11)		32
Total	**(all out, 60 overs)**		**198**

Barnes 27-9-51-7 Dolman 4-1-19-0 Jagger 10-3-28-0
Ryan 19-5-68-3

Wales 1st innings

NVH Riches	c Roach	b Constantine	12
D Boumphrey		b Francis	6
CA Rowland		b Constantine	6
CN Bruce	run out		10
A Ratcliffe		b Neblett	71
VA Metcalfe	c Rae	b Neblett	18
ST Jagger	c Neblett	b Francis	30
CE Dolman	c Neblett	b Browne	35
SF Barnes	not out		25
WH Rowland		b Browne	0
FP Ryan	c&b	Browne	0
Extras	(b 6, lb 6, nb 4)		16
Total	**(all out, 63.5 overs)**		**229**

Francis 17-4-70-2 Scott 4-0-19-0 Constantine 14-4-44-2
Browne 15.5-6-26-3 Neblett 13-2-54-2

West Indies 2nd innings

G Challenor	lbw	b Barnes	26
CA Roach	c Ryan	b Barnes	30
WH St Hill	c Ratcliffe	b Ryan	7
*+RK Nunes		b Barnes	17
OC Scott	c Ryan	b Barnes	4
CR Browne	lbw	b Ryan	1
LN Constantine	c Jagger	b Ryan	16
EA Rae		b Ryan	11
JM Neblett	lbw	b Ryan	2
CV Wight	c Riches	b Barnes	1
GN Francis	not	out	0
Extras	(b 17, lb 3, nb 2)		22
Total	**(all out, 41.1 overs)**		**137**

Barnes 21-5-67-5 Jagger 5-0-31-0 Ryan 15.1-6-17-5

Wales 2nd innings (target: 107 runs)

NVH Riches	c Browne	b Francis	4
D Boumphrey		b Constantine	4
CA Rowland	not out		52
CN Bruce	not out		42
Extras	(b 4, lb 1)		5
Total	**(2 wickets, 22.5 overs)**		**107**

DNB: A Ratcliffe, VA Metcalfe, ST Jagger, CE Dolman, SF Barnes,
WH Rowland, FP Ryan.

Francis 4-0-29-1 Constantine 2-0-15-1 Scott 3.5-0-28-0
Browne 9-2-9-0 Neblett 4-0-21-0

MATCH NO. 19

West Indies in England, 1928

Test arena. Not only was he popular with the players, but he had substantial popular support. Unlike Captain Nunes of the West Indies, Percy was a player's man, always intimate with their concerns and keen to support them on and off the field. He was a colourful character, described as debonair off the field, and as a dashing, free-hitting, left-handed bat on the field. On the eve of the first Test match he was confident that his men would dispose of the West Indians without any protracted struggles.

A.F.P. Chapman, England's captain.

The West Indies team was equally predictable. Led by Nunes, it included Wight, Bartlett, Browne, Challenor, Constantine, Fernandes, Francis, Griffith, Hoad, Martin, Neblett, Rae, Roach, Scott, St. Hill and Small. The team lacked a spinner of quality, and with a pace attack not supported by slower wickets, England appeared confident of its ability to contain the tourists.

The First Four-Pronged Pace Attack

The West Indian strategy, in the face of a strong English batting line-up, was to rely to a greater degree on its four-pronged pace attack. No specialist spinner was taken on tour, and it was commonly believed that there was none of world class in the West Indies. The battalion of fast bowlers had shown its worth in the 1923 tour and the decision was taken to treat the English to a little more of the same. No other Test team carried such bowling ammunition. The West Indians were pioneering this new method, and at the dawn of its Test status declared its hand by endorsing unrelenting speed as its technology of choice.

The firepower was placed in the hands of Learie Constantine, Herman Griffith, George Francis and Joe Small.

THE 1928 ARCHIVES

WALES IN WINNING POSITION

At the end of yesterday's play in the match between Wales and the West Indies, at Llandudno, Wales, with eight wickets in hand, required 75 runs for victory.

Rain delayed the resumption of play till nearly half-past 12, and stopped cricket later on, but good progress was made. With four wickets in hand, Wales began the day 32 behind their opponents' total, and Ratcliffe and Dolman continued their unbroken partnership till they had added 60 in less than three-quarters of an hour. The West Indies' score was passed with three wickets standing but at 1 o'clock rain fell and the game could not be continued till 20 minutes to 3. Then, in 20 minutes, the last three men were dismissed for 25 runs, the innings closing for 229, a lead of 31 runs. Browne caused the breakdown after luncheon, taking the last three wickets in three overs and five balls for four runs. Going in a second time, Challenor and Roach cleared off the arrears in a quarter of an hour, thanks to the enterprise of the latter, who scored 30 out of the 32 realized by the opening partnership. Challenor had the good fortune to be missed three times, but after driving Jagger over the screen, he was l-b-w at 66, and Hill left at the same total. At tea-time, with Nunes and Scott together, the board showed 73 for three wickets. With three runs added afterwards, two wickets went down, and half the side were out for 76. Constantine then hit out, driving Barnes on to the Pavilion roof, and Rae later hit the same bowler over the ropes in helping Nunes to put on 23, but the innings closed for 137, so that Wales were left to make only 107 to win.

–The Times,
Friday, July 27, 1928, Page 6

A group of West Indies players from which the team to meet Warwickshire at Edgbaston on Saturday next will be selected.

—*The Sunday Mercury, Sunday, 8 July, 1928, Front Page*

A Nation Imagined

This was the optimal combination of experience and young talent. Francis, Small and Constantine had already made an impression on the 1923 tour to England, and were, therefore, veterans of the conditions. Griffith was the newcomer. But what a character he was! Born in Trinidad of Barbadian parents, Herman was brought back to Barbados as a child and grew up in the ranks of the fiercely competitive schoolboys' cricket culture. As a teenager he was known as a speedster with extraordinary stamina, aggression, and control. He was always one to express his opinions on the game forcefully, as with any other matter beyond the boundary, and many of his fans and friends believed that this explained his non-selection for the 1923 tour. As that was effectively the decision of Captain H.B.G. Austin, the Barbadian merchant mogul, it was an easy matter to see

George Headley swinging his bat.

THE 1928 ARCHIVES

Leicestershire v West Indies
Aylestone Road, Leicester - 28, 30, 31 July, 1928 (3-day match)

Result: Match drawn
Umpires: WR Cuttell and D Denton

Leicestershire 1st innings
GBF Rudd		b Constantine	23
AW Shipman	c Browne	b Griffith	22
NF Armstrong	lbw	b Griffith	7
GL Berry	run out		55
JC Bradshaw	c Constantine	b Small	6
WE Astill		b Griffith	22
+TE Sidwell	c Small	b Constantine	59
CAR Coleman	c Nunes	b Griffith	1
H Riley		b Constantine	8
HC Snary	not out		10
HA Smith	c St Hill	b Constantine	5
Extras	(b 6, lb 3, nb 1)		10
Total	**(all out, 69.4 overs)**		**228**

Griffith 22-7-62-4   Constantine 20.4-4-75-4   Small 10-0-28-1
Browne 14-3-32-0   Martin 3-0-21-0

West Indies 1st innings
G Challenor	c Riley	b Astill	50
CA Roach		b Shipman	4
FR Martin	c Snary	b Coleman	20
WH St Hill	lbw	b Astill	0
*+RK Nunes	c&b	Astill	42
MP Fernandes	c Sidwell	b Smith	37
LN Constantine	c Riley	b Smith	50
ELG Hoad	not out		21
JA Small	lbw	b Snary	2
CR Browne	c Riley	b Coleman	1
HC Griffith	st Sidwell	b Astill	21
Extras	(b 15, lb 5, w 2, nb 1)		23
Total	**(all out, 88.4 overs)**		**271**

Shipman 5-0-9-1   Astill 26.4-5-68-4   Coleman 21-4-49-2
Snary 21-6-58-1   Smith 15-2-64-2

Leicestershire 2nd innings
GBF Rudd		b Constantine	0
AW Shipman	c Browne	b Small	74
NF Armstrong	lbw	b Martin	64
GL Berry	lbw	b Martin	19
JC Bradshaw	lbw	b Small	0
WE Astill	c Griffith	b Browne	2
+TE Sidwell	c Roach	b Martin	3
CAR Coleman		b Griffith	0
H Riley	not out		19
HC Snary	not out		1
HA Smith	c Browne	b Griffith	1
Extras	(b 4, lb 11)		15
Total	**(9 wickets declared, 93 overs)**		**198**

Griffith 18-8-34-2   Martin 29-12-38-3   Small 23-4-43-2
Browne 16-4-34-1   Constantine 7-2-34-1

West Indies 2nd innings (target: 156 runs)
CA Roach	c Smith	b Snary	18
ELG Hoad	not out		12
WH St Hill		b Snary	0
JA Small	not out		7
Extras	(lb 2)		2
Total	**(2 wickets, 11 overs)**		**39**

DNB: G Challenor, FR Martin, *+RK Nunes, MP Fernandes, LN Constantine, CR Browne, HC Griffith.

Coleman 3-1-12-0   Snary 5-1-12-2   Armstrong 3-0-13-0

MATCH NO. 20
West Indies in England, 1928

why popular opinion on the island held that he was a victim of class and racial prejudice on that occasion.

George Francis was the man preferred by Captain Austin. Described as a gentleman off the field, he kept ahead of the social game that Griffith was learning the hard way. Big George, unlike Herman, came from the most economically disenfranchised section of the Barbadian working class. He worked on the ground staff of the Pickwick Club at its Kensington Oval home. This was the club of the merchant elite, and gracious George, a practice bowler to Austin and the other great ones, was identified as a man capable of terrorising the English with the steep climb of his length balls. Batsmen, it seemed, were always unsure whether to play forward or back when George had the new ball. His selection for the 1928 tour was expected. In fact, it was anticipated that he would have the historic honour of bowling the first West Indian Test ball, and he did.

Herman Griffith,
—*The Sporting Chronicle*, Tuesday, August 14, 1928

The West Indian imagination, however, featured Constantine as its hero in the confrontation with English batting. Considered the most improved player since 1923, Constantine was rated as the fastest in the quartet. At age 27, compared with Griffith, 35, and Francis, 31, his quickest deliveries were said to bedazzle batsmen, wicket-keepers, and slip fielders. At home he was the superstar of the emerging game. In 1923, English crowds flocked to see him bat, bowl and patrol the cover area. He was already hailed as the greatest all-round cricketer the region had produced, and by the end of the tour he had cinched a claim to being the best in the world.

West Indians expected that he would share the new ball with Francis. English batsmen who faced them in 1923, and had heard reports of their substantial improvement, had good cause to be concerned. Backing up would be Griffith

EVEN PLAY AT LEICESTER

The match between Leicestershire and the West Indies at Leicester on Saturday was watched by the biggest crowd seen on the ground this season. The county, batting first, scored 228, and then dismissed four of the West Indies batsmen for 95.

Leicestershire, who made their runs in three hours and three-quarters; were chiefly indebted to Berry and Sidwell, who between them were responsible for exactly half their side's total, and it was only a brilliant return from the cover-point by Roach that got rid of Berry when he indeed, fielded extremely well throughout the innings, and mention must also be made of Constantine's catch at point which dismissed Bradshaw. Though generally good, the West Indies bowling came in for severe punishment at times, Constantine being hit for three successive 4's by Berry, and Sidwell treating Martin in the same way. Griffith came out with the best figures, taking four wickets for 62 runs, while Constantine had four for 75.

The West Indies began badly, losing Roach at 12. Martin, who stayed to make 20, was missed at slip 10 runs later. Challenor and Martin then scored steadily, sending up 50 in 65 minutes, and Challenor completed an excellent 50 before being caught by Riley. Martin left at 90, however, and with St. Hill failing to score, the West Indies, at the close, were 133 behind with six wickets to fall.

–The Times,
Monday, July 30, 1928, Page 5

WEST INDIES LEAD

The West Indies accomplished a good performance yesterday at Leicester in gaining a first innings lead of 43 runs over the county side, for they began the day 13 behind with four of their best men out.

They owed something to the mistakes of their opponents in the field. Fernandes, who helped to add 82 for the fifth wicket, being twice missed – by Astill in the gully and by Armstrong at slip – off Smith's bowling. Constantine, coming in at the fall of the fifth wicket, scored 50 in 25 minutes. At luncheon the West Indies were no more than 20 runs on with nine men out, but the last wicket gave some trouble, Hoad and Griffith both scoring freely. At the conclusion of the innings, which lasted for four hours and ten minutes, rain set in, and at 5.15 it was decided to abandon play for the day.

–The Times,
Tuesday, July 31, 1928, Page 7

and Small, and in their pairing as a combination resided the hopes for the West Indies team. The versatile C.R. 'Snuffie" Browne was cast in the role of back-up bowler. West Indians knew that Snuffie had an effective leg spin and googly, and could bowl medium-fast seamers if called upon. Martin and Scott, deemed all-rounders on the side, were reserved bowlers. Scott, especially, had a moderate reputation for slow

O.C. Tommy Scott

THE 1928 ARCHIVES

Somerset v West Indies
Recreation Ground, Bath - 1, 2, 3 August, 1928 (3-day match)

Result: Match drawn
Umpires: EF Field and TW Oates

West Indies 1st innings
G Challenor	lbw	b Hunt	1
CA Roach	c White	b Hunt	0
FR Martin	lbw	b Greswell	5
ELG Hoad	c Longrigg	b White	26
EA Rae	st Luckes	b White	11
MP Fernandes	c Longrigg	b White	30
JA Small	c Earle	b Greswell	9
*CV Wight	c Madden	b White	9
CR Browne		b Greswell	25
GN Francis		b Greswell	5
HC Griffith	not out		1
Extras	(b 2, lb 6)		8
Total	**(all out, 86.3 overs)**		**130**

Hunt 24-8-29-2   Wellard 4-1-6-0   Greswell 23.3-10-35-4
White 33-14-50-4   Young 2-1-2-0

Somerset 1st innings
JCP Madden	c Challenor	b Martin	16
A Young	lbw	b Francis	7
+WT Luckes	c&b	Francis	0
RA Ingle	c sub	b Martin	29
GE Hunt	c&b	Small	32
JCW MacBryan	not out		84
*JC White		b Martin	3
EF Longrigg	c Fernandes	b Small	13
AW Wellard		b Small	1
GF Earle		b Small	15
WT Greswell	c Fernandes	b Martin	3
Extras	(b 11, lb 1, nb 1)		13
Total	**(all out, 78 overs)**		**216**

Francis 19-6-46-2   Griffith 9-3-27-0   Martin 30-7-78-4
Small 20-5-52-4

West Indies 2nd innings
G Challenor	c Madden	b Greswell	10
CA Roach		b Greswell	17
ELG Hoad	c&b	Greswell	71
FR Martin	lbw	b Wellard	31
EA Rae	lbw	b Greswell	0
MP Fernandes	c White	b Wellard	36
JA Small	c MacBryan	b Wellard	0
CR Browne		b Greswell	14
*CV Wight	not out		24
GN Francis		b Wellard	0
HC Griffith	not out		14
Extras	(b 5, lb 8)		13
Total	**(9 wickets, 118 overs)**		**230**

Hunt 12-3-19-0   Greswell 42-17-68-5   Wellard 34-10-59-4
White 30-9-71-0

MATCH NO. 21

West Indies in England, 1928

and medium swing bowling. Older Jamaicans remembered his match figures of 11 for 138 in a game against the MCC tourists in the 1910-11 tour; and younger ones spoke of his outstanding success against the Tennyson team in 1926-27. In the matches he played, Scott returned figures of 4-81, 6-75, 4-65, and 8-67.

Most West Indian batsmen, too, were selected on the basis of significant reputations at home and abroad. It was a star filled team, though placed in the hands of arguably one of its weakest players. Captain Nunes was classified as a reasonable left-handed batsman with some experience of English conditions. He played for Surrey's second XI in the 1919 season, and was vice captain to Austin on the 1923 tour, where he failed to distinguish himself. A graduate of the prestigious Dulwich College, his educational achievements gave him a distinct advantage in the leadership selection process. For this reason he was called upon by the WICBC to lead onto the field men of greater cricketing ability and experience. He did, however, press his claim on the field with a fine innings of 200 not out and another of 108 against Lord Tennyson's side.

To the extent that there was opposition on the team towards his leadership, the focus was more on his aloofness with persons he considered of an inferior social class and race than his form as a batsman. Some observers, however, did express the opinion that his leadership would pose significant problems for this very reason. His inability, or refusal to see to it that his young countryman, George Headley, who, more than any other, had devastated Tennyson's bowlers, was presented as evidence of things not seen but known.

There were no players of Indian ancestry on the side. Blacks had fought their way into the first-class cricket world, first by securing access to the bowling department where players from the elite social strata could not hold their own or were willing to relinquish space in the face of a superior display. Headley, in 1928, was the main contender for the coveted position of star batsman on the team. The absence of Indian players seemed phenomenal, even more so when it is considered that someone with the skill of Sonny Ramadhin was the first to enter, but not until as late as 1950. The culture of class and race discrimination was clearly hurting Indian cricketers deeper into the twentieth century, and the projection of the West Indies Test team in 1928 as a multi-ethnic outfit, without Indian players, suggested

SOMERSET LEAD WEST INDIES

GOOD INNINGS BY MACBRYAN

At the close of play in the match between Somerset and the West Indies at Bath yesterday the visitors, with four wickets down in their second innings, were only 32 runs ahead of Somerset's first innings total of 216.

A fine innings by J.C.W. MacBryan enabled Somerset to gain a lead of 86 on the first innings. Somerset, in reply to the visitors' total of 130, had scored 15 and lost two wickets on Wednesday, and they met with a further setback yesterday when Gaskell was out to a catch at mid-off with 10 runs added. Hunt then hit out, scoring two 4's and a 6 in one over from Martin, and he and Ingle improved matters by putting on 45 in 35 minutes. Then MacBryan came in. He made runs at a brisk rate from the moment he reached the wicket, but for some time could find no one to stay with him. The West Indies total, however, was passed with four wickets standing, and MacBryan completed 50 in an hour and a quarter during a partnership with Longrigg which realized 55 in 45 minutes. Earle later drove vigorously, obtaining 14 runs from Small in the over in which he was bowled, and the Somerset innings, having lasted three hours 35 min., closed for 216.

The visitors started their second innings badly, Greswell disposing of Challenor and Roach with 27 runs on the board. It took Hoad half an hour to open his score, and he proceeded with much care afterwards. Martin and Rae left at 72, but with Fernandes as partner Hoad saw the arrears wiped off and the 100 appeared when the innings had lasted an hour and 35 minutes.

–The Times,
Friday, August 3, 1928, Page 6

–The Times, Thursday, August 2, 1928, Page 5

RAIN PREVENTS FINISH AT BATH

Rain prevented cricket at Bath yesterday till a quarter to 3 and spoiled the possibility of an interesting finish to the match between Somerset and the West Indies, which had to be left drawn. The West Indies at the drawing of stumps stood 144 ahead with one wicket to fail.

Hoad and Fernandes proceeded quietly with their fifth-wicket partnership, but before the latter, having batted well for an hour and a half, was caught at first slip, the total had been increased by 67. Wickets fell at intervals, but Hoad – who was most unenterprising in his methods – completed his 50 in three hours, and before giving Greswell a return catch he put together a score of 71. This effort extended over four hours and included only five boundary hits, but though it proved valuable in placing his side beyond all question of defeat, it caused frequent "barracking" from the spectators. Wight and Griffith shared in a bright last-wicket stand, Griffith hitting Greswell out of the ground, and the pair were still together at the close.

–The Times,
Saturday, August 4, 1928, Page 6

that the social and political democratising process was far from complete.

Nunes's Jamaican teammate, F.R. Martin, had an altogether different set of credentials. He was rated as a skilful left-handed batsman with an appetite for big scores. In his first major first-class game for Jamaica against Barbados in 1924, he impressed with a massive 195 not out, and in the Tennyson tour he demonstrated his world class with a polished 204 not out for Jamaica. Martin had won the right to open the innings with the legendary Challenor, and West Indians expected great things from this partnership.

Lord Tennyson

M.P. Fernandes and W. St. Hill were selected to join Captain Nunes in the middle order. Although they did not constitute as strong a middle order as England's, these two players were known in the West Indies to be sound and reliable, and the best that was available. Fernandes was selected as a replacement for G.A. Dewhurst, the wicket-keeper, also from Guiana. He had toured in 1923, but did not excel on account of ill health, though he managed to finish second in the first-class batting averages largely because of the 110 against Leicestershire, and two innings of 49 and 73 against Lancashire. He batted well with Small in the lower middle, where they made partnerships of 102 and 131. His 124 against Trinidad, and 120 against the MCC in the 1925-26 season, cemented his place on the team. He was expected to bat at number three.

St. Hill, the free-hitting Trinidadian, also had an impres-

THE 1928 ARCHIVES

Glamorgan v West Indies
St Helen's, Swansea - 4, 6, 7 August, 1928 (3-day match)

Result: Match drawn
Umpires: EF Field and JH King

West Indies 1st innings

G Challenor	c Mercer	b Bates	55
FR Martin	lbw	b Arnott	9
ELG Hoad	lbw	b Ryan	22
EL Bartlett		b Ryan	11
*+RK Nunes	not out		127
MP Fernandes		b Mercer	4
LN Constantine		b Mercer	20
OC Scott		b Arnott	13
CV Wight		b Mercer	21
JA Small		b Arnott	19
GN Francis		b Bates	3
Extras	(b 12, lb 11)		23
Total	**(all out, 100.2 overs)**		**327**

Mercer 29-5-94-3   Arnott 17-2-50-3   Ryan 25-2-76-2
Clay 11-4-30-0   Bates 12.2-1-43-2   Davies 6-2-11-0

Glamorgan 1st innings

WE Bates	c Francis	b Scott	49
JT Bell		b Small	25
AH Dyson	c Martin	b Small	0
NVH Riches	lbw	b Small	65
MJL Turnbull		b Small	0
*T Arnott		b Small	15
D Davies	lbw	b Francis	30
JC Clay		b Scott	33
J Mercer	c Small	b Scott	1
FP Ryan	c Fernandes	b Constantine	3
+D Sullivan	not out		4
Extras	(b 23, lb 6, nb 2)		31
Total	**(all out, 93 overs)**		**256**

Francis 12-3-26-1   Martin 12-3-33-0   Constantine 7-2-27-1
Small 31-13-52-5   Scott 31-6-87-3

West Indies 2nd innings

G Challenor	c Davies	b Ryan	47
FR Martin	lbw	b Ryan	9
ELG Hoad	st Sullivan	b Ryan	21
EL Bartlett	c Sullivan	b Davies	4
*+RK Nunes		b Ryan	10
MP Fernandes	c Mercer	b Ryan	0
OC Scott	c Davies	b Ryan	7
LN Constantine		b Arnott	19
CV Wight	c&b	Mercer	9
JA Small	not out		15
GN Francis	c Clay	b Ryan	6
Extras	(b 8, lb 9)		17
Total	**(all out, 51.4 overs)**		**164**

Mercer 15-2-41-1   Arnott 9-1-36-1   Ryan 19.4-7-62-7
Davies 8-3-8-1

Glamorgan 2nd innings (target: 236 runs)

WE Bates	c Francis	b Constantine	2
JT Bell	c Constantine	b Small	36
AH Dyson		b Small	11
NVH Riches	not out		28
MJL Turnbull	not out		14
Extras	(b 8, lb 2)		10
Total	**(3 wickets, 37.5 overs)**		**101**

DNB: *T Arnott, D Davies, JC Clay, J Mercer, FP Ryan, +D Sullivan.

Francis 3-1-6-0   Scott 4-1-8-0   Martin 12-4-33-0
Small 15.5-9-25-2   Constantine 3-0-19-1

MATCH NO. 22

West Indies in England, 1928

sive 1925-26 domestic season. His 105 against the MCC preceded an aggressive 144 in the first of the trial matches. In the third trial game his 44 and 71 were sufficient to secure his selection. There were many sceptics, however, to whom the St. Hill selection was controversial. Yet, his performance in the regional competitions batting at number three had been undeniably impressive. Against Barbados in 1925 at Queen's Park, he top scored with 66 and 64, and against Guiana he scored 100 and 0. During the critical 1927 season, he compensated for the 0 and 18 against Barbados by scoring the first century in the trials. He silenced the critics, who then turned their attention to the selection of Roach (Trinidad) and Rae (Jamaica). Neither could claim selection as a right based on performance in the trial matches. Rae was able to put together a tortured 80 for the 'Rest of the West Indies' against Barbados, and Roach came in with 84 for the combined Trinidad-Guiana team against Jamaica in the first match.

More compelling was the selection of Hoad, the 32-year old Barbadian who had scored a match-winning 150 not out against Jamaica in 1924-25, and 115 against Guiana. These were followed in 1925-26 by 174 not out against Trinidad, and 123 run out against Leeward Islands. In the third trial match he scored 153 for Barbados against the Rest of the West Indies, and with Tarilton, secured a partnership of 238 in the second match. In addition, his 8-33 against Antigua in 1926-27 signalled his arrival at the regional level as a useful slow bowler. Much less can be said

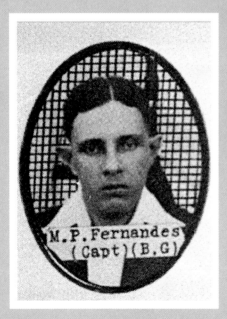

CENTURY BY R.K. NUNES

For the first time in first-class matches during the tour, R.K. Nunes, the West Indies captain, made a century at Swansea on Saturday, and thanks mainly to this, the touring team, batting for nearly five hours, put together a total of 327. In reply to this, Glamorgan scored 33 without loss.

Challenor's steadiness prevented the possibility of an early breakdown in the batting, that batsman staying in for over two hours in scoring a faultless, if somewhat sedate, 55. Nunes, going in at the fall of the third wicket at 85, began quietly, taking an hour and a half to complete his 50, but once he exceeded that figure he batted entertainingly. Constantine, having made 20 inside a quarter of an hour, was out rather unluckily. He tried to hit to leg a bad-length ball from Mercer, but missed the ball, which, striking him on the shoulder, rolled on to the stumps. Nunes remained to the end of the innings and in all scored 127.

In the last half-hour of the day Bates and Bell batted steadily without being parted.

–The Times,
Monday, August 6, 1928, Page 4

GOOD GAME AT SWANSEA.

Although Glamorgan met with an early setback in the match against the West Indies at Swansea yesterday a fine innings by N. V. H. Riches enabled them to effect a recovery, and in the end the home county did well to get to within 71 runs of their opponents' total of 327. The cricket throughout the day was marked by great keenness and was thoroughly enjoyed by a company of fully 18,000 people.

Bates and Bell had scored 33 without loss, so that Glamorgan were 294 runs behind. Small with successive deliveries dismissed Bell and Dyson, but, although Bates took half an hour to score five, Riches made a number of excellent strokes to reach his 50 in an hour and a half. The partnership for the third wicket had produced 98 when Bates, playing a defensive stroke, was surprised to see Francis effect a catch by taking the ball almost off the bat.

Constantine was unable to bowl after

—The Times, Tuesday, August 7, 1928, Page 5

RYAN'S FINE BOWLING.

Just when it was expected that there would be an interesting finish to the match between Glamorgan and the West Indies at Swansea yesterday, rain set in and the game had to be abandoned as a draw.

When the West Indies continued their second innings yesterday morning, with the score at 86 for five wickets, O. C. Scott was soon caught at cover-point, but L. N. Constantine came in to hit 4's off the first two deliveries he received. He had scored four boundaries in making 19 in ten minutes, before T. Arnott knocked his middle stump out of the ground. Ryan was handicapped by an injury to his back, but in taking seven wickets at a cost of a shade under nine runs apiece, he accomplished easily his best performance of the season. Subsequently, Bell and N. V. Riches batted soundly for Glamorgan, who were favourably placed when the game had to be given up.

Score :—

—The Times, Wednesday, August 8, 1928, Page 5

about J. Neblett and C.V. Wight, the vice-captain, though O.C. Scott's supporters believed that the 35-year-old was second only to Constantine as the team's genuine all-rounder.

There were no surprises, then, when England elected to bat after Captain Chapman won the toss. As predicted by some, England took off at a rate in excess of a run per minute, and reached a total of 401 in just over a day. The 122 by Tyldesley showed that the West Indies' pace attack lacked penetration, even though Constantine's four for 82 from 26 overs, and Griffith's two for 78 from 29 overs, indicated persistently tight control of length and line.

England's performance was a solid one. Sutcliffe's 48, batting at number one, and the captain's 50 at number six, in addition to Hammond's 45 at number four, confirmed the opinion that it would be an enormous challenge for West Indian bowlers to cut through the batting order. Hammond and Tyldesley recovered from the early pace assault, and launched a counter-attack that saw 77 runs scored in 50 minutes. It was an intimidating response that signalled to the other batsmen that West Indian pacers could be contained. More than raw pace was required. Tyldesley had survived a confident lbw call from a well-disguised slower ball from Constantine before he had scored, but soon the bowling seemed predictable and repetitive. Browne was economical but wicket-less, bowling 22 overs for 53 runs. Small initially came in for some stick, but settled, finishing with two for 67 off 15 overs.

The collapse of the West Indies batting for a total of 177, 74 runs short of being asked to follow on, was due not to the fiery pace of Larwood, who broke down with injury, but to the guile of the spinners. Freeman bagged two for 40 in the first innings and Jupp four for 37. In the second innings, the West Indies were 44 for six before the end of the second day's play, but the tail wagged, and the last four batsmen added 122 runs, with Small, batting at number eight, becoming the first cricketer in a West Indies Test team to

THE 1928 ARCHIVES

Gloucestershire v West Indies
Royal & Sun Alliance County Ground, Bristol - 8, 9, 10 August, 1928
(3-day match)

Result: Match drawn
Umpires: J Stone and W Cooper

Gloucestershire 1st innings
AE Dipper		b Constantine	25
CCR Dacre		b Constantine	6
WR Hammond	c&b	Scott	32
RA Sinfield	c&b	Constantine	4
FJ Seabrook	lbw	b Scott	76
+H Smith		b Small	20
WL Neale	not out		66
CJ Barnett	c Nunes	b Scott	5
CWL Parker	c Wight	b Constantine	14
*WH Rowlands	c&b	Neblett	19
PT Mills	c Hoad	b Scott	26
Extras	(b 10, b 16)		26
Total	**(all out, 104 overs)**		**319**

Griffith 17-2-57-0 Small 23-5-50-1 Constantine 22-5-66-4
Scott 25-0-61-4 Martin 9-0-32-0 Neblett 6-2-16-1
Roach 2-0-11-0

West Indies 1st innings
CA Roach	c Hammond	b Parker	71
ELG Hoad	c Hammond	b Sinfield	0
HC Griffith	run out		4
*+RK Nunes	c&b	Hammond	71
EL Bartlett		b Hammond	36
FR Martin	c Barnett	b Sinfield	53
LN Constantine	lbw	b Hammond	17
JM Neblett		b Neale	27
JA Small		b Parker	18
OC Scott	c Hammond	b Parker	66
CV Wight	not out		19
Extras	(b 12, lb 3, nb 2)		17
Total	**(all out, 138.3 overs)**		**399**

Sinfield 33-11-91-2 Mills 31-12-52-0 Hammond 28-1-93-3
Barnett 3-0-7-0 Neale 6-0-17-1 Parker 37.3-13-122-3

Gloucestershire 2nd innings
AE Dipper	not out		62
RA Sinfield		b Griffith	3
WR Hammond		b Scott	24
FJ Seabrook	c sub	b Griffith	26
WL Neale	not out		7
Extras	(b 5, nb 2)		7
Total	**(3 wickets, 57 overs)**		**129**

DNB: CCR Dacre, H Smith, J Barnett, CWL Parker, *WH Rowlands, PT Mills.

Griffith 15-6-23-2 Small 21-8-45-0 Scott 13-2-40-1
Martin 6-2-12-0 Neblett 1-0-1-0 Roach 1-0-1-0

MATCH NO. 23

West Indies in England, 1928

> **WEST INDIES AT BRISTOL.**
> At the close of the first day's play in the match between Gloucestershire and the West Indies at Bristol yesterday, the West Indies, with nine wickets to fall, were 312 runs behind.
> The pitch was easy paced, but at the beginning of the Gloucestershire innings L. N. Constantine bowled extremely well. The total was only seven when he got through C. C. Dacre's defence with a ball that came quickly from the pitch. Hammond made a number of powerful drives, but having scored 32 out of 47, he drove a ball hard and low, and was brilliantly caught by the bowler. At 68 Con-

—The Times, Thursday, August 9, 1928, Page 5

score half a century. His 52 did not prevent his team from losing by an innings and 58 runs after reaching the embarrassing total of 166.

In the first innings, Larwood's pace proved no major challenge for Challenor and Martin, who posted a respectable opening partnership of 86. With Challenor gone, however, the collapse was immediate: two for 86, three for 88, four for 95, five for 96, six for 122 and seven for 123. In the second innings, the spinners again did the damage, with Freeman taking four for 37 and Jupp, three for 66. Challenor's duck in the second innings, as well as

Ernest Tyldesley, one of the English batsmen who impressed.

Constantine's, ripped what was left of the spirit from the batting line-up.

The comprehensive failure of West Indies batting – the highest score being Martin's 44, might have surprised many spectators who saw good starts squandered by indiscretion.

The massive defeat in the first Test required an immediate West Indian response, from the batsmen in particular.

WEST INDIES' LEAD

For the greater part of the day at Bristol yesterday the West Indies' batsmen were engaged in a keen struggle for runs against steady Gloucestershire bowling. L.N. Constantine failed, but C.A. Roach, R.K. Nunes, and F.R. Martin all batted well, and, with an innings completed on either side, the visiting team let by 80 runs.

The West Indies had lost one wicket for 17 runs and, with H.C. Griffith run out in Sinfield's first over, it was only natural that Roach and Nunes batted with care. Roach however, soon got the measure of the bowling, and, driving and cutting well, he reached his 50 inside an hour. Eventually out to a good catch at slip, Roach made his 71 out of 113 in an hour and 25 minutes. He hit no fewer than 11 fours. Another productive partnership followed between Nunes and Bartlett, the latter hitting well all round the wicket.

By luncheon time the pair had increased the score to 168, and a separation was not effected until the stand had produced 60 for the fourth wicket. At 212 Nunes returned a ball to Hamond, after batting for three hours and hitting six fours. Constantine made two boundaries during his brief stay, while Martin, when 32, had the good fortune to be missed by Dipper.

–The Times,
Friday, August 10, 1928, Page 6

—*The Sporting Chronicle, Tuesday, August 14, 1928, Front Page*

A NATION IMAGINED

The next match was scheduled against Northamptonshire. Determined to show that their spirits were not broken by the circumstances at Lord's, the West Indians, in a show of player power, crushed the county side by an innings and 126 runs. Challenor scored a polished 97, and Constantine showed no mercy with an aggressive 107 that saw balls flying great distances beyond the boundary. In addition, when he picked up the new ball, Northamptonshire batsmen had no answer to his pace. He finished with match figures of 13 for 112. In the next match against Nottinghamshire, Bartlett finally came good with 109, and in the last game before the second Test against Worcestershire, a West Indian batting feast ended on a score of 410 for six. Hoad struck form with 149 not out, but Worcestershire's reply of 439 for two, led by 200 not out by Gibbons, again signalled that all was not perfect with the bowling attack.

Second Test

The second Test started at Old Trafford, Manchester, on Saturday July 21. Three changes were made to the English side which had won the first Test. Hobbs, Elliott and J.C. White took the places of Hallows, Smith and Larwood. But the result was much the same; England winning by an innings and 30 runs. The explanation, in part, was due to the inability of the batsmen to perform to their ability on placid wickets. According to *The Times*:

> "In our first Test Match at Lord's, the West Indies gave the impression that their batting strength is not sufficient to give them any real chance of beating England under equal conditions. The deficit is of temperament rather than technique, and will be less apparent as their experience grows. But at present their batsmen, with the exception of G. Challenor and R.K. Nunes, are easily lured on big occasions into adopting tactics which the bowlers, particularly the slow bowlers, desire to impose upon them, and their judgement in running is elementary." [*The Times*, July 23, 1928.]

The West Indies won the toss and batted first. Once again a solid opening partnership was not consolidated by the middle order. Roach was promoted to the opening position with Challenor, and they comfortably reached 48 for the loss of the first wicket. Roach reached the second fifty in a Test for the West Indies before he was lbw to Freeman, Challenor running out himself at 24. Again, Constantine

THE 1928 ARCHIVES

Third Test - England v West Indies

The Oval, London, England - 11, 13, 14 August, 1928
England won by an innings & 71 runs

West Indies 1st innings
G Challenor	c WR Hammond	b M Leyland	46
CA Roach		b H Larwood	53
FR Martin	c APF Chapman	b AP Freeman	25
*+RK Nunes		b MW Tate	0
EL Bartlett		b H Larwood	13
OC Scott	c G Duckworth	b MW Tate	35
LN Constantine	c APF Chapman	b WR Hammond	37
CV Wight	c APF Chapman	b MW Tate	23
JA Small	lbw	b AP Freeman	0
HC Griffith	not out		0
GN Francis	c APF Chapman	b MW Tate	4
Sundries	BY: 2 LB: 0 NB: 0 WD: 0 PN: 0		2
Total	RR: 2.98 runs/6 balls		**238**

FoW: 1-91, 2-112, 3-113, 4-132, 5-160, 6-177, 7-231, 8-234, 9-234, 10-238

H Larwood 21-6-46-2   MW Tate 21-4-59-4   AP Freeman 27-8-85-2
WR Hammond 8-0-40-1   M Leyland 3-0-6-1

England 1st innings
JB Hobbs	c JA Small	b GN Francis	159
H Sutcliffe		b GN Francis	63
GE Tyldesley	c LN Constantine	b HC Griffith	73
WR Hammond	c JA Small	b HC Griffith	3
M Leyland		b HC Griffith	0
EH Hendren	c CA Roach	b HC Griffith	14
*APF Chapman	c LN Constantine	b HC Griffith	5
MW Tate	c HC Griffith	b GN Francis	54
H Larwood	c GN Francis	b GN Francis	32
+G Duckworth		not out	7
AP Freeman	c GN Francis	b HC Griffith	19
Sundries	BY: 1 LB: 2 NB: 6 WD: 0 PN: 0		9
Total	RR: 4.22 runs/6 balls		**438**

FoW: 1-155, 2-284, 3-305, 4-305, 5-310, 6-322, 7-333, 8-394, 9-413, 10-438

GN Francis 27-4-112-4   FR Martin 2-1-9-0   LN Constantine 20-3-91-0
OC Scott 14-1-75-0   JA Small 15-2-39-0   HC Griffith 25.5-4-103-6

West Indies 2nd innings
G Challenor	c WR Hammond	b AP Freeman	2
CA Roach		b H Larwood	12
FR Martin		b MW Tate	41
*+RK Nunes	c EH Hendren	b H Larwood	12
EL Bartlett	c H Larwood	b AP Freeman	8
OC Scott	c G Duckworth	b H Larwood	4
LN Constantine	c H Larwood	b MW Tate	17
CV Wight	not out		12
JA Small	c AP Freeman	b MW Tate	2
HC Griffith	c WR Hammond	b AP Freeman	5
GN Francis	c WR Hammond	b AP Freeman	4
Sundries	BY: 6 LB: 4 NB: 0 WD: 0 PN: 0		10
Total	RR: 2.45 runs/6 balls		**129**

FoW: 1-12, 2-26, 3-46, 4-59, 5-70, 6-102, 7-102, 8-110, 9-123, 10-129

H Larwood 14-3-41-3   MW Tate 13-4-27-3   AP Freeman 21.4-4-47-4
WR Hammond 4-2-4-0

MATCH NO. 24

West Indies in England, 1928

Clifford Roach

failed with the bat, making four following scores of 21 by Martin at number three, St. Hill, three at number four, Hoad, 13 at number five, and Captain Nunes, 17 at number six. Once again, the bowlers were called to the fore. Browne (23) and Scott (32), batting at numbers eight and nine

THIRD TEST MATCH

WEST INDIES DISMISSED FOR MODERATE TOTAL

A.P.F. CHAPMAN'S FOUR CATCHES

The third and last of the series of Test matches this season between England and the West Indies was begun at the Oval to-day. England having already won at Lord's and Old Trafford, each time in a single innings, the issue of the rubber was already determined. R.K. Nunes won the toss, and the West Indies took first innings. They made a moderate start, scoring 130 for the loss of three wickets before lunch.

The innings closed for 238, seven wickets falling in a hundred minutes after lunch for the addition of 108 runs. Tate was the most successful bowler, with four for 59. A.P.F. Chapman, after one bad miss, made four brilliant catches.

With glorious weather favouring the contest, some 6,000 or 7,000 people had assembled to see the start at half-past eleven. The England team differed in four instances from that victorious at Old Trafford, Leyland, Larwood, Duckworth, and Hendren. Taking the places of Jupp, J.C. White, Elliott, and D.R. Jardine, the last of whom, being compelled to cry off, was replaced by Hendren. In the West Indies eleven, C.R. Browne, E.L.G. Hoad, and W. St. Hill gave way to E.L. Bartlett, C.V. Wight, and J.A. Small.

The visitors opened the batting with G. Challenor and C.A. Roach, and soon after half past eleven Larwood sent down the first ball from the Vauxhall end, and in this over Tate distinguished himself by a small piece of fielding at short leg. Tate bowled from the other end, and the first ball nearly dismissed Roach...

Except for one snick by Roach, which sent the ball safe and clear of the fieldsmen, the batting of both men was sound and confident. Roach made some nice strokes on the leg-side, and off-drove well, though the old fault of running dangerously sharp runs was still in evidence. At 29 Freeman went on for Larwood, and Tate, at 49, gave way to Hammond, off whom Roach, with a 3 to the on, sent up 50 in less than fifty minutes. Freeman had Roach missed off him by Chapman at mid-off when 34 and with the total at 52, the England captain making a sad muff of an easy chance. Otherwise, Freeman was scored off pretty freely, both batsmen driving hard and playing the Kent man quite easily. Roach completed 50 out of 88 in sixty-five minutes, but Larwood came on again at 91 and bowled him first ball, the West Indies man playing at it with a cross bat. Hitting four 4's, Roach made 53 out of 91 in seventy minutes.

At starting, Roach looked like being out quite early, for he flicked at the off ball too much, but, having settled down, he batted extremely well. Martin joined Challenor, and the game quietened down, Martin being in for fifteen minutes before scoring. The 100 went up in rather more than an hour and a half, and 2 runs later Tate resumed bowling.

Leyland bowled at 107, and in his first over, Challenor, at 112, after batting extremely well for an hour and forty minutes, tried to cut the ball and was caught in the slips. It was rather a sad ending to a good display. Nunes went in next, but did not enjoy a very long stay, for, with a single added, he was bowled by a ball that looked to turn quickly and just sufficiently to beat the bat. Larwood went on again for one over before lunch, but no further wicket fell, the score being 130 for three wickets at the interval (Martin 17 and Bartlett 42).

Glorious weather prevailed when promptly at 2.15 cricket was continued before a company which now numbered about 16,000. Freeman and Larwood bowled, and in the former's first over Bartlett nearly played on. Then from the first ball from Larwood, Bartlett had his off stump sent flying, the score being 132.

Scott joined Martin and was nearly bowled first ball, while Martin put up a ball from Freeman only just short of Hammond at slip. Larwood was bowling very well and neither batsman seemed at all comfortable in dealing with him.

Martin and Scott, however, settled down to better cricket, Scott getting right to the pitch of the ball to drive Freeman, and the partnership began to look quite promising when, at 160, Martin, who had been in 80 minutes, was out to a fine catch...

Scott continued to play very well, his method of dealing with Freeman being excellent. In one over he scored nine off the Kent bowler. The English fielding was good, Hendren doing one glorious piece of work. Then, at 177, Scott, who had been in three-quarters of an hour, was cleverly caught rather low down at the wicket.

Constantine made one good half-arm hook for 4 off Tate, but in the latter's next over he should have been out, Hammond in the slips missing him badly. Constantine had then made 7, and the total was 190. The 200 went up in three hours and ten minutes. Hammond, going on at 205, Constantine hit him for three 4's in his first over. Twice after that, following a short break while refreshments were taken out, Constantine scored four 4's off Hammond, but at 231 he skied the ball over the bowler's head, and Chapman, running from mid-on brought off a clever catch. Constantine hit six 4's during his stay of 45 minutes, and the partnership reached 54 in half an hour.

–The Birmingham Mail,
Saturday, August 11, 1928, Page 5

respectively, saw the team to the modest total of 206. Again, the spinners were the most destructive, with Freeman improving his figures with the first five-wicket haul. The West Indies batsmen had no answer, and his five for 54 off 33.4 overs said it all. Jupp chipped in with two for 39 off 18 overs.

Sutcliffe played them with determined mastery.

The second innings' collapse to 115 all out was again the result of the work by Freeman. His second five-wicket collection, this time off 18 overs at a cost of 39 runs, exposed the weakness of the West Indies batting. The two openers, Challenor and Roach, scored ducks, falling to the seamers of Hammond and Tate. England's 351 was more than enough. Sutcliffe's 54, Hammond's 63 and Jardine's 83 wore down a West Indian bowling attack that was not expensive, but lacked penetration.

THE THIRD TEST MATCH
ENGLAND'S ADVANTAGE

The Oval was a good place on Saturday, and its amenities were enjoyed by some 20,000 discriminating persons who in the third Test Match saw England, after experiencing a certain amount of anxiety during the first two hours of play, establish what, humanly speaking, must be a winning advantage over the West Indies.

It is widely believed that the public is deeply interested in the results of first-class cricket matches. The fact that so large a number of spectators paid doubled entry money to watch the third match of an already decided rubber makes one wonder whether that belief is well founded. The probable truth is that those who have cricket in their blood are impelled by the urge of the bacillus to be present when the most instructive and entertaining players of the game are on view, be the importance of the result achieved great or small. On Saturday there were a dozen cricketers answering to that description engaged at the Oval, 11 Englishmen and L.N. Constantine. Most of the Englishmen, notably A.P.F. Chapman as captain and Hobbs as the star batsman, played their parts satisfactorily, and Constantine was commendably successful in providing the comic relief. We were pleasantly tickled when Hobbs took a short single off his bowling, and Constantine, charging down the pitch, first threw down the wicket unnecessarily and then retrieved his own overthrow from the other side.

One's impression at the end of the day's play was that the course of it had been influenced by incidents of slip-fielding more than by anything else. In this connexion Chapman's captaincy is open to a little adverse criticism. He did not insist that Tate and Larwood should do without a long-leg, at least so long as the shine was on the ball, and place an extra man in the slips. Before play had been in progress more than ten minutes C.A. Roach had scored two 4's by upper cuts, either of which might have cost him his wicket if England's captain had relied entirely on his own judgment in the placing of the field. Later when the England bowlers were beginning to establish mastery three missed chances in the slips postponed success. Finally Chapman finished off the innings by making two barely possible catches which compensated for the previous mistakes. Then, when England went in, Sutcliffe was thrice missed behind the wicket. He gave his first chance when he had made but one run. Had it been accepted the effect on an admittedly emotional team like the West Indies might have been highly beneficial.

The ground was quite firm, but lifeless after recent showers, when R.K. Nunes won the toss and sent in G. Challenor and C.A. Roach to face Larwood and Tate. Challenor was not destined to make a hundred, but only a great batsman can play as he played. Roach brought off a number of fine strokes all round the wicket, but his judgment was sadly at fault. He persisted in attempts to make the stroke which schoolboys are warned to avoid because "it counts out if you hit the ball." Twice, as has been said, he scored four by means of it. On the other occasions he failed to establish connexion between bat and ball. When Freeman came on for Larwood both men dealt with him firmly and decisively, though Chapman should have caught Roach at mid-off for him. Four square off drives at his expense by Challenor were the strokes of a heaven-sent dream. Roach gave a difficult chance at the wicket off Tate, and twice tried ineffectually to run his partner out; each time Sutcliffe at mid-off was at fault....

Freeman was doing no good against F.R. Martin, a left-handed batsman who gives himself plenty of time to play his strokes, and Challenor. So Tate relieved him. The rate of scoring now became very slow, but no wicket fell before the moment to rest Larwood arrived. Then Leyland went on and Challenor, going for his square off-drive, slightly mistimed his stroke, and sent the ball hard and low towards short slip. Hammond in that position can stand abnormally close to the bat, and he took what would hardly have been a chance to less quick-sighted slip fieldsmen. Nunes was at once beaten by a very good ball from Tate, but Martin and E.L. Bartlett tided over the awkward 20 minutes before luncheon stylishly and profitably.

After the interval Larwood's first ball beat Bartlett, who was half-way through his stroke when his stumps were hit. Freeman shared the bowling with Larwood, and the pair kept Martin and O.C. Scott very quiet for half an hour. During this period Scott crouched to his stroke and took the ball high up on his bat. Suddenly he began to stand up and run in to drive Freeman. But before he could be taken off Freeman got a lucky wicket. He gave Martin a full pitch which the batsman hit to square-leg with all his power. Chapman, standing by the umpire, took the catch quite easily, as a man must if he is not himself to be taken to the hospital.

This should have been the beginning of the end, for Hammond ought to have caught Constantine at slip off Tate, even if the ball did touch Duckworth's gloves in passing. Constantine also survived an attempt to match Freeman in cleverness, and then began to hit. Tate should have had him caught by Freeman in the gulley just after Duckworth had taken Scott at the wicket, and Freeman might also have caught C. V. Wight in the same place off the same bowler. Constantine hit Hammond harder and more frequently than any other bowler, but lost his wicket to him.

–The Times,
Monday, August 13, 1928, Page 7

Hammond scored 63 in the Second Test.

Francis (23-4-68-0), Constantine (25-7-89-1) and Griffith (25-7-69-3) bowled with "sustained ferocity", but Hobbs and Sutcliffe played them with determined mastery. Browne's two for 72 off 25, however, indicated the value of accurate length and line bowling. He dismissed the dangerous Hobbs for 53, and Tyldesley for three. The scars of defeat showed everywhere on the West Indies team. That they were humiliated seemed clear enough, though the unfavourable weather condition was considered a significant factor in their defeat by the more generous elements within the media. For sure, the next game, played against Wales, a team with no significant credentials, indicated the depth to which morale had fallen.

Furthermore, it showed the weakness of Captain Nunes as a leader. His aloofness and inability to lead beyond the boundary, became an even larger liability for the team. Beaten by the Welsh at Llandudno by eight wickets, following the earlier disgrace at Dublin at the hands of the Irish, they could do no better than secure draws in subsequent games against Leicestershire, Somerset, Glamorgan and Gloucestershire. Captain Nunes, 127 not out against Glamorgan, seemed far too little, too late for his team mates who approached the third and final Test with spirits down, if not out.

THE 1928 ARCHIVES

ENGLAND'S WINNING POSITION

(FROM OUR CRICKET CORRESPONDENT.)

England secured the lead of 200 on the first innings against the West Indies at the Oval yesterday, which was the minimum of achievement which could be considered adequate, having regard to the position in which the game stood when the day's play started. But the result accomplished was more satisfactory than the manner of its accomplishment.

After Hobbs was out several of his successors played as if they did not relish the pace of the bowling which they had to face. Very likely, if the match had been one against Australia the batsmen would have risen to the occasion. But facts are facts. And the fact is that after the fall of the second wicket until Larwood came in, we saw no one, except for a few minutes A.P.F. Chapman, resolutely throw his left foot to the line of the fast bowling regardless of consequences. As might be expected, uppish strokes in the slips ensued, and in the afternoon the West Indians were in the mood to hold their catches. But in the first half-hour of the morning they gave themselves a lot of trouble by twice missing Hobbs.

HOBBS' STAMINA

Hobbs survived to complete another of his many remarkable innings. This time it was the physical and moral stamina of the man as much as the technical beauty of his strokes which excited wonders of admiration. He was tired out on Saturday night and one day's rest had obviously been insufficient to restore all his normal vigour. Out in the middle he could not trust himself to time a full drive, and refrained from attempting the stroke even when a tempting half-volley came along. When he came back to the pavilion at half-past 12 he looked pale and haggard, as if bed was the proper place for him. Yet he had scored almost twice as fast as Tyldesley, who is one that looks for runs and knows how to get them; and he had omitted no opportunity to run a sharp single or to turn a long one into two.

The showers which fell on Sunday and on Monday morning had had no apparent effect on the pitch, which remained of the pace that allows the batsmen to play forward or back at will to balls of doubtful length, and the fast bowlers had to pitch quite short if they wanted the ball to bump. But the rain which interrupted play about half-past 12 did later cause the ball to come along at two heights and varying paces. While conditions were at their easiest Hobbs and Tyldesley scored fast. Tyldesley made most of the boundary hits, but Hobbs excelled in placing his strokes on both sides of the wicket.

Nunes is a very watchful captain, who is inclined to overdo carefulness in placing his field. While Hobbs was in the onside fielders were constantly changing their positions to suit his stroke. The changes were quite ineffectual, as he merely steered the ball where the fielders were not. When the rain came England were only three runs short of the West Indies' total. Play was not resumed until 2.30. Hobbs had now been in for about three hours and a half, and he could no longer resist the temptation to drive. The result was a couple of fours over slip's head. Finally, he pulled a short ball from Francis, hard and straight to short leg, where J.A. Small hung on to it creditably.

ENGLISH BATTING FAILURES

After this H.C. Griffith, from the Vauxhall end, enjoyed an hour of complete triumph. If the wicket was beginning to help him he made full use of its assistance. If the batsmen contributed to their own downfall by meeting him diffidently, he did nothing to inspire them with courage. Tyldesley was the first to go, nicely caught at third slip off a weak stroke, made too far from a rising ball. Hammond, strangely un-aggressive, skied the ball the first time he tried to hit. The next ball jumped to Leyland's elbow and came down on to his stumps. Hendren, after making some good strokes off O.C. Scott's leg-breaks, played short at a fast ball outside his off-stump and edged it to slip. Chapman indiscreetly played a forcing back-stroke at a rising ball that might have been left alone.

At this point seven wickets were down for 340. Tate and Larwood then retrieved the situation. Tate's manner of retiring to short leg and sparring at the ball suggested that he was appealing to the fast bowlers for mercy. But from the curious positions which he assumed he cut and hooked with tremendous power. Larwood, by way of contrast, batted immaculately, and made his runs by long, fluent strokes, played with his feet correctly placed.

C.A. Roach and G. Challenor went in a little before 5.30 to attack the adverse balance of 200. Roach wiped off 10 in Larwood's first over with three beautiful leg-strokes. But Larwood was bowling yards faster than he had done on Saturday and with much more fire. In his second over a break-back shattered Roach's wicket. At the other end Tate opened with four maiden overs. Clearly Chapman is one who believes in quick changes of bowling. He soon had Larwood off, put Freeman on at the Pavilion end, and let Tate change to the other. The tactics worked, for Challenor in trying to drive a leg break edged it to slip.

The two left-handers, F.R. Martin and Nunes, showed some signs of sticking in, so Freeman changed ends and Larwood had a second spell. Larawood had Nunes well caught at third slip, and E.L. Bartlett, who shaped well, pulled a drive to mid-on. It looks as if nothing but rain could save the West Indians to-day.

–*The Times*,
Tuesday, August 14, 1928, Page 5

A NATION IMAGINED

Leyland (batting and inset), was selected for the Third Test.

Third Test

For the third Test, which started at the Oval on Saturday, August 11, England again made three changes to the side, with Leyland, Larwood and Duckworth (the wicket-keeper) replacing J.C. White, V.W.C. Jupp and Elliot. The team was selected with the Australian tour in mind, all members being assured of the trip 'down under'. Although the English team had already begun preparing their minds to meet the Australians, they had no difficulty defeating the West Indies for the third time by an innings.

The West Indies left out St. Hill, who had top-scored in the second innings of the second Test; Hoad, who had failed in both innings, and Browne. Bartlett came in to bat at number five, and Small was brought back. This was to no avail. The West Indies could not be revived. The record of defeat, *The Times* noted, served to establish "a record of disappointment which may stand unbroken for all time". [August 15, 1928.] The West Indies, though, posted an improved first innings total of 238, with an impressive opening partnership of 91 in 70 minutes by Challenor (46) and Roach (53). The captain's duck, and Bartlett's 13 meant that the opening performance was eroded by the collapse to 160 for five. Scott, promoted from number nine to number six, made a defiant 35, and Constantine made his highest score of the series when he was caught in the slips by Chapman off Hammond

VALUE OF TESTS
BOWLING HOPES

The series of Test cricket matches between England and the West Indies have been of high value to both teams in the opinion both of Mr. Chapman, the English skipper, and Mr. Nunes, the West Indies captain.

To the home side the value lies in the opportunities the matches have afforded for preparing the players for Australian Tests; to the visitors they have been of great practical worth and encouragement.

It was interesting to learn in an interview yesterday that if reports form Australia represent the true position of affairs, Mr. Chapman does not think his men will find so much difficulty with fast bowling "down under" as they have experienced at the hands of Griffith, Francis, and Constantine.

"The Test matches have done a great amount of good in interesting England in choosing their team for Australia," said the English captain.

"Moreover I have had three opportunities of getting to know my side and welding it into something of a machine in the way of fielding.

"We have had the opportunity of playing some really good fast bowling which was more varied than that we expect to encounter in Australia that is, if we can rely upon the accounts to hand from "down under."

"These matches have been fought out in the most pleasant sprit, and I feel sure they have done West Indies cricket a great deal of good. "It is to be hoped that the M.C.C. will be able to send out a really strong team to engage in the return series."

Mr. Nunes said: "I, as the first West Indies Test match skipper, and the rest of the team should in no way be disheartened by the result of the three Test matches, though I am somewhat disappointed that there was no necessity for England to bat in the second innings of any Test match."

"The experience will benefit West Indies cricket in the same way as Test matches benefited Australia and South Africa when they were in their infancy in such cricket.

"As far as I can gather, with the exception of the bowling of McDonald and Gregory in 1921 England has not batted since the war against a better attack, and if we had had the luck of the game in the field the scores might have been much smaller.

"Anyhow I am extremely proud that in no Test match did we fail to bowl out all the English eleven.

"I hope when the M.C.C. visit the West Indies in the winter of 1929-30 the strongest possible team will be sent, not only because it will help cricketers to play the best of England but also will give the opportunity of seeing many of England's great cricketers whose reputations have spread throughout the small but loyal colonies of the Empire.

"I am not without hope, and I have every reason from past experience to think that England will not win the Test matches under conditions to which our players are accustomed by an innings and runs."

–The Sporting Chronicle,
Wednesday, August 15, 1928, Front Page

ENGLAND WIN AGAIN
A QUICK FINISH

(FROM OUR CRICKET CORRESPONDENT.)

The West Indies lost the third Test Match at the Oval yesterday, as they lost the first two, by an innings, thereby establishing a record of disappointment which may stand unbroken for all time, and certainly cannot escape notoriety in these days, when the study of statistics is so intense. Their six outstanding wickets went down yesterday for 68 runs, of which something like one-third were scored by snicks through the slips. They were made to work for the remainder of them, for England's captain drove home his advantage relentlessly, and endeavoured to win in the minimum of time by the widest possible margin.

Their latest failure provides no reason for modifying the opinion previously expressed, that the tale of disappointment is due to faults of temperament rather than of technique. It also provides little ground for hoping that experience gained during their tour has done much to eradicate these faults from all the members of the party. L.N. Constantine's case is regrettably typical. The batting and bowling averages indicate that he is one of those cricketers who may be described as half a side in himself. At the present moment he is less, not more, likely to merit that description on a big occasion than he was two months ago. He is an acrobatic fieldsman, but sacrifices accuracy to the display of antics. Thereby he wastes something of the energy which it is the bounden duty of a fast bowler to conserve. He throws fast and hard, and shows off his power in season and out of it, so that his colleagues, in particular the wicket-keeper, must put in a lot of unnecessary work to save overthrows. He wins a certain amount of applause from the ring by these tricks, but the judicious, including his captain, grieve.

–The Times,
Wednesday, August 15, 1928, Page 6

for 37. England's 438, built around an outstanding innings of 159 by the incomparable Hobbs, and supported by Sutcliffe (63), Tyldesley (73) and Tate (54), again demonstrated the inexperience of West Indies bowling at the Test level. Griffith's six for 103 from 25.5 overs was nonetheless important. The one batsman he bowled, Leyland, scored a duck, batting at number five. The other five batsmen were caught from defensive fielding positions.

The West Indies' second innings of 129 reflected the general pattern that English spectators had come to expect. The inability to master spin bowling found expression in Freeman's four for 47 off 27 overs. Tich Freeman was in his element in 1928, and West Indies batsmen, like county players, had no proper response to top spinners and the googly. In the 1928 season, Freeman had taken 304 wickets for Kent; the West Indies players were just unfortunate to be caught in his web.

After the Oval match, the West Indies team fell to pieces. Defeated by an innings at the hands of Sussex, they could only manage a draw against Hampshire. Martin's 165 against the 'Hamps' was followed by Browne's 103 against Kent, who they defeated by 201 on account, in large measure, of the 11 for 118 match figures recorded by Griffith. Whatever the flicker of hope for a face-saving performance was dashed when the Harlequins smashed the bowlers all over The Saffrons Park in amassing 676 for eight declared.

The critical moment for the West Indians was the mind-shattering defeat in the second Test. Prior to this match the team had been performing moderately well. They had won four first-class matches and lost four, not at all a disgraceful performance. From then, however, results showed the effects of diminishing enthusiasm and growing fatigue. Eight matches were lost and just one victory secured. No longer were there any brilliant performances amidst team defeats. All seemed lost. Hoad, 145, in the penultimate game against Sir Julian Cahn's XI, and 124 in the final game against Leveson-Gower's XI, seemed like generous farewell gestures from bowlers not motivated to score points against opponents already tumbling.

Sussex v West Indies
New County Ground, Hove, Brighton - 18, 20, 21 August, 1928 (3-day match)

Result: Sussex won by an innings & 87 runs
Umpires: A Morton and J Moss

West Indies 1st innings
G Challenor	lbw	b Bowley	44
CA Roach		b Wensley	22
FR Martin	c&b	JH Parks	0
WH St Hill	st Cornford	b Wensley	7
*+RK Nunes		b Wensley	0
EL Bartlett		b JH Parks	6
LN Constantine		b JH Parks	6
CV Wight		b JH Parks	40
CR Browne	c Grimston	b JH Parks	1
GN Francis	c Hollingdale	b Wensley	26
HC Griffith	not out		34
Extras	(lb 2)		2
Total	**(all out, 78 overs)**		**188**

Wensley 31-15-60-4   Browne 6-3-9-0   Gilligan 4-1-17-0
JH Parks 24-12-44-5   Bowley 8-2-23-1   Wagener 5-0-33-0

Sussex 1st innings
EH Bowley	c Wight	b Martin	62
JH Parks		b Constantine	25
HW Parks		b Constantine	5
RA Hollingdale	lbw	b Browne	28
KA Sellar		b Constantine	1
GS Grimston	lbw	b Browne	52
AF Wensley		b Griffith	22
JG Wagener	not out		80
*AER Gilligan		b Browne	12
+WL Cornford	c Browne	b Martin	53
FBR Browne	c sub	b Browne	0
Extras	(b 10, lb 4, nb 10)		24
Total	**(all out, 113.4 overs)**		**364**

Francis 9-2-21-0   Griffith 28-9-68-1   Constantine 25-4-103-3
Browne 33.4-5-81-4   Martin 15-3-52-2   Roach 3-0-15-0

West Indies 2nd innings
G Challenor	c Grimston	b Wensley	7
CA Roach	c Cornford	b Browne	2
FR Martin	not out		26
WH St Hill	c HW Parks	b Browne	0
*+RK Nunes	lbw	b Bowley	1
EL Bartlett	c Grimston	b Wensley	7
LN Constantine	lbw	b Wensley	20
CV Wight	c Hollingdale	b Wensley	0
CR Browne		b Wensley	5
GN Francis	st Cornford	b Bowley	1
HC Griffith	c Hollingdale	b Wensley	8
Extras	(b 9, lb 3)		12
Total	**(all out, 41.5 overs)**		**89**

Wensley 17.5-3-44-6   Browne 13-2-16-2   JH Parks 5-4-50
Bowley 6-3-12-2

7.

Reflections on a Journey

Before the beginning of the third Test, *The Times* had concluded that "so far the West Indies have hardly proved themselves able to justify their promotion to Test Match rank." [August 11, 1928.] By the end of the Test, the paper was able to inform its readers that the West Indies' "latest failure provides no reason for modifying the opinion previously expressed, that the tale of disappointment is due to faults of temperament rather than of technique". [August 15, 1928.]

At the end of the tour, the West Indies had lost the three Tests by an innings each, and had been defeated by Ireland, the Minor Counties, Yorkshire, Warwickshire, Wales, Sussex, the Harlequins, an England XI and H.D.G. Leveson-Gower's XI; a total of twelve losses. They had defeated Derbyshire, Cambridge University, Middlesex, Northamptonshire and Kent; a total of five wins. Thirteen matches were drawn against Essex, Surrey, Oxford University, MCC, Yorkshire, Lancashire, Nottinghamshire, Worcestershire, Leicestershire, Somerset, Glamorgan, Gloucestershire and Hampshire.

Cricket historian, Keith Sandiford, had described the 1928 team as the weakest in West Indian Test history. Its senior players, Challenor (40), Browne (38), Small (36), Griffith (35), Martin (35), St. Hill (35), Nunes (34), Fernandes (31) and Francis (31), had all passed their peak. It would have been a more formidable force had Test status been granted for the 1923 tour. It was hardly surprising that the most consistent players were Constantine (27) and Roach (24).

Their highest Test score was 238, and in six innings the team secured more than 200 runs only twice. *The Sporting Chronicle* of August 15, used its front page to celebrate the "hat-trick of Test Match victories", and to pronounce that it had been an "ill-fated elevation" of the West Indies team to

THE 1928 ARCHIVES

WEST INDIES FAIL AT BRIGHTON

Although the team that Sussex put in the field against the West Indies at Brighton on Saturday was by no means representative, they gained a considerable advantage as a result of the day's play. They dismissed their opponents for 188, and, scoring 111 for the loss of four batsmen, stood at the end of the day only 77 behind with six wickets to fall.

At one time it seemed that the West Indies would be dismissed for a far smaller total, for, although G. Challenor and C.A. Roach scored 38 for the first wicket, eight wickets were down soon after luncheon for 98. From that point, however, the batting showed improvement, the last two wickets producing 90 runs. J. Parks bowled extremely well, taking half the wickets for less than nine runs each.

Bowley and J. Parks gave Sussex a good start by sending up 50 in as many minutes, but at 54 L.N. Constantine got rid of J. Parks and six runs later also bowled H. Parks. Bowley, however, prevented the possibility of a breakdown, During the course of his innings he completed his 2,000 runs for the season, and, before being third out at 102, scored 60 in two hours, with eight 4's, chiefly powerful drives or leg hits, as his chief figures.

–The Times,
Monday, August 20, 1928, Page 5

—The Sunday Mercury, Sunday, 22 July, 1928, Front Page

Test status. Totting up the figures for the matches, they calculated that as England had scored a total of 1,190 in three innings as compared with the West Indies tally of 1,031 in twice as many, the team was "not yet fitted" for Test rank.

Yet for the West Indies, Hoad had topped the batting averages on tour with 36.42, and Constantine had performed the double, 107 wickets (22.95 av.) and 1,381 runs (34.52 av.). The bowlers had done reasonably well in the Tests. They achieved a reputation for pace and fury that impressed spectators. Bowlers Constantine, Small and Griffith had made a profound impact upon English cricket, and had signalled the arrival of a West Indian fast-bowling culture.

The batting department, however, failed consistently. No West Indian batsman scored a Test century. The first of three fifties was made by fast bowler J.A. Small. His 52 in the first Test was bettered by C.A. Roach, who compiled 53 in the first innings of the third Test, after his even 50 in the first innings of the second Test. Roach, then, just 24 years old, the youngest batsman on the tour, was the only one to shine. Constantine was the single player to finish the tour with an enlarged reputation. He was the man in demand. When he signed a contract to play for Nelson in the Lancashire League, West Indians felt mixed emotions. Many were happy to see another West Indian star working the professional circuits of England, while others lamented his loss to West Indian playing fields. That he was a Test failure paled to insignificance when the spectacular county performances were recalled and assessed. He became the first cricketer, other than an Australian, to make the double in first-class cricket on a tour to England.

Rae, who had impressed in the West Indies, failed to secure a double-figure average, and Challenor was a shadow of his 1923 self. Hoad's two end-of-tour festival centuries gave him the misleading lead average of 36.42. His overall failure as a batsman meant that Martin, who was the most consistent in the Tests, with the second tour average of 32.61, was really the pick of the batsmen.

The Exclusion of George Headley

Against the background of the Test defeat were rumours throughout the West Indies that George Headley, the enormously radiant star, should have been included. All who

Hampshire v West Indies
County Ground, Southampton - 22, 23, 24 August, 1928 (3-day match)

Result: Match drawn
Umpires: WR Cuttell and H Thompson

Hampshire 1st innings
G Brown		b Constantine	0
AS Kennedy		b Constantine	12
R Aird	c Martin	b Constantine	19
CP Mead	lbw	b Constantine	11
AL Hosie		b Griffith	26
JA Newman	c Constantine	b Challenor	118
*LH Tennyson	c Hoad	b Browne	217
GS Boyes	c Constantine	b Scott	11
+WH Livsey		b Browne	0
AK Judd	not out		2
RPH Utley	c Wight	b Challenor	0
Extras	(b 6, lb 5, nb 2)		13
Total	**(all out, 123.2 overs)**		**429**

Griffith 22-3-89-1   Browne 35-6-103-2   Constantine 28-3-93-4
Scott 21-2-66-1   Martin 8-5-10-0   Challenor 9.2-2-55-2

West Indies 1st innings
CA Roach		b Kennedy	84
FR Martin	c Aird	b Boyes	165
ELG Hoad	lbw	b Boyes	51
CR Browne		b Newman	38
G Challenor		b Newman	0
*+RK Nunes	lbw	b Boyes	10
MP Fernandes	c Mead	b Newman	23
LN Constantine	st Livsey	b Boyes	19
OC Scott	not out		7
CV Wight		b Newman	0
HC Griffith	c Aird	b Boyes	0
Extras	(b 5, lb 6, w 2, nb 3)		16
Total	**(all out, 137.2 overs)**		**413**

Utley 20-1-66-0   Kennedy 27-11-71-1   Newman 36-15-73-4
Judd 7-0-56-0   Boyes 35.2-9-91-5   Brown 8-0-35-0
Hosie 4-2-5-0

Hampshire 2nd innings
G Brown	c Challenor	b Constantine	19
R Aird	c Wight	b Constantine	14
AK Judd	not out		0
*LH Tennyson	not out		23
Extras	(b 5, lb 1)		6
Total	**(2 wickets, 16 overs)**		**62**

DNB: AS Kennedy, CP Mead, AL Hosie, JA Newman, GS Boyes, +WH Livsey, RPH Utley.

Constantine 8-0-31-2   Challenor 8-2-250

MATCH NO. 26

West Indies in England, 1928

George Headley

THE 1928 ARCHIVES

HAMPSHIRE'S RECOVERY
BIG INNINGS BY MAJOR TENNYSON

After a poor start Hampshire made a splendid recovery against the West Indies at Southampton yesterday and, although play was interfered with by rain and bad light, the county scored 312 for the loss of half their wickets.

The earlier Hampshire batsmen found the bowling of L.N. Constantine so difficult that half the side – four of them to the fast bowler at a cost of 24 – were out for 88 runs. The West Indies had no further success, however, Newman and Major Tennyson engaging in a capital stand which completely altered the course of the game.

Hampshire's misfortunes began when, with a single scored, Brown was bowled in Constantine's first over, and, although Kennedy tried to force the game, he was bowled at 18. R. Aird and Mead increased the score to 44 before rain caused a slight delay. With the fall of the fifth wicket Tennyson joined Newman. The scoring for some time was extremely slow, but when the batsmen had become thoroughly set the total was increased at a splendid pace. The Hampshire captain punished H.C. Griffith for a series of 4's, and with three hits to the boundary off successive deliveries from that bowler he reached his 50, which Newman accomplished a little later.

The bowling was completely collared after the tea interval, Tennyson hitting with great vigour. A drive for 6 brought the partnership to 200, and, although he gave E.L.G. Hoad a chance which the fieldsman failed to hold, Tennyson continued to hit hard. When, at 20 minutes to 6, an appeal against the light resulted in stumps being drawn, the total stood at 312, the partnership for the sixth wicket having produced 224 in three hours and a half.

–The Times,
Thursday, August 23, 1928, Page 6

–*The Sporting Chronicle, Monday, August 13, 1928, Front Page*

saw him in action in Jamaica in 1927 recommended that he be selected for the first Test team. Headley was born in Panama in 1909 of a Barbadian father and Jamaican mother. He did not go to Jamaica until the age of ten, following a stay of four years in Cuba where his parents had migrated in search of work. As a teenager, his cricket ability was the subject of village tales, and he was invited to join the St Catherine Cricket Club where his first-class game developed.

When Lord Tennyson's XI arrived in Jamaica in 1927, Headley, just 18, was selected to play against it for Jamaica. In one game he scored 211 out of 348, and reports circulated throughout the West Indian cricketing world that a batting genius had been found. The forces of white supremacy that claimed batsmanship as its privilege and special preserve in West Indian cricket showed no keenness to select the young Headley for the inaugural Test tour. He continued, however, to impress against touring English sides while dominating local bowlers in colonial contests. The thrashing received by the Test team in England in 1928 opened the opportunity for new players to be admitted, and George Headley was selected to make his Test debut against England in the 1929-30 West Indian tour.

Headley's arrival was, in some respects, quite revolutionary. The first specialist batsman hailing from the black working classes in West Indies Test cricket, he was sent in to bat at number three: no black player could reasonably expect to bat this high in the Test batting order. These were esteemed positions reserved for the plantocracy and its mercantile allies. The lower social orders were presumed to occupy corresponding positions in the batting line-up, and the public understood this as the natural order of things beyond the boundary. Headley's coming, then, was welcomed by the working classes as the sign of things to come – the beginning of the democratic process that would turn the colonial world upside down. From his teammates, he was charged with holding up the batting department against the English bowling attack and with removing the possibility of another humiliating whitewash.

The Barbadian-Jamaican-Panamanian did not disappoint. In the first Test at Bridgetown, January 11-16, 1930, he scored 21 and 176 in the drawn game. The second innings score of 176 runs was made in a total of 384. The debutant was proclaimed immediately by West Indians as their best batsman, and the player who symbolised the journey ahead for the nation imagined.

Kent v West Indies
St Lawrence Ground, Canterbury - 25, 27, 28 August, 1928 (3-day match)

Result: West Indies won by 201 runs
Umpires: LC Braund and RD Burrows

West Indies 1st innings
CA Roach	c GJ Bryan	b Ashdown	6
FR Martin	c Wright	b Marriott	25
ELG Hoad	lbw	b Marriott	14
G Challenor		b Wright	64
*+RK Nunes		b Wright	11
MP Fernandes	lbw	b Freeman	10
LN Constantine	lbw	b Marriott	30
CR Browne		b Freeman	103
OC Scott		b Wright	3
JM Neblett		b Ashdown	0
HC Griffith	not out		5
Extras	(b 5, lb 6)		11
Total	**(all out, 73.2 overs)**		**282**

Wright 15-3-73-3   Ashdown 10-2-48-2   Freeman 25.2-6-87-2
Marriott 23-4-63-3

Kent 1st innings
HTW Hardinge		b Griffith	38
WH Ashdown		b Constantine	2
FE Woolley		b Constantine	2
+LEG Ames	c Scott	b Griffith	6
JL Bryan	c Fernandes	b Griffith	14
JA Deed		b Browne	13
GJ Bryan		b Griffith	1
*GB Legge	not out		30
AP Freeman		b Browne	5
AC Wright	c Browne	b Griffith	10
CS Marriott		b Griffith	0
Extras	(lb 6)		6
Total	**(all out, 37.3 overs)**		**127**

Griffith 15.3-3-57-6   Browne 5-3-5-2   Constantine 17-1-59-2

West Indies 2nd innings
CA Roach	c Legge	b Freeman	19
FR Martin		b Wright	82
ELG Hoad	c Hardinge	b Freeman	15
G Challenor		b Freeman	11
*+RK Nunes		b Freeman	3
MP Fernandes	c Woolley	b Freeman	13
LN Constantine	c GJ Bryan	b Freeman	0
CR Browne		b Freeman	18
OC Scott	c Hardinge	b Freeman	1
JM Neblett	c Ashdown	b Freeman	21
HC Griffith	not out		20
Extras	(b 5, lb 8)		13
Total	**(all out, 75.5 overs)**		**216**

Wright 18-5-36-1   Ashdown 3-0-16-0   Freeman 34.5-8-104-9
Marriott 20-4-47-0

Kent 2nd innings (target: 372 runs)
HTW Hardinge	c Constantine	b Griffith	4
WH Ashdown	c Neblett	b Constantine	2
+LEG Ames		b Griffith	0
JL Bryan	not out		95
GJ Bryan		b Constantine	9
JA Deed	c Fernandes	b Griffith	1
*GB Legge	c Neblett	b Griffith	9
AP Freeman	c Constantine	b Browne	22
FE Woolley	c Neblett	b Griffith	5
AC Wright	c Fernandes	b Constantine	5
CS Marriott		b Constantine	7
Extras	(b 8, lb 2, nb 1)		11
Total	**(all out, 50.3 overs)**		**170**

Griffith 19-2-61-5   Browne 9-3-36-1   Constantine 22.3-5-62-4

Appendix

The West Indies Cricket Guide

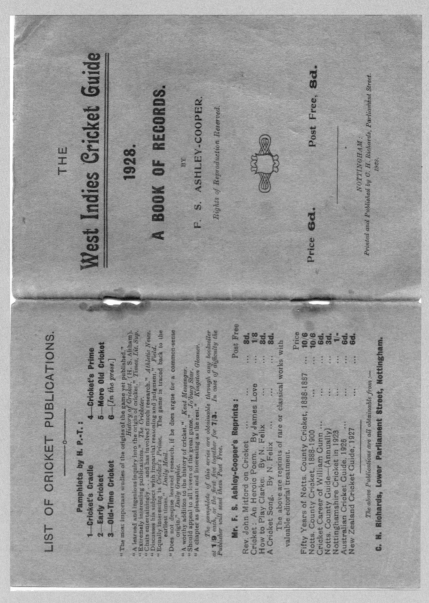

This 28-page booklet was issued to mark the tour. It carried some historical information on the game as played in the West Indies, including tours to and from the islands, dating as far back as 1857. It featured brief profiles of the team, "Anglo-West Indian Records," and "Some West Indian Records." It also listed 36 of the matches they played on the tour. The following pages are taken from the tour guide.

WEST INDIES AT CANTERBURY
GOOD ALL-ROUND DISPLAY

The West Indies proved a big attraction at Canterbury on Saturday, and at the close of play Kent, with two wickets to fall, were 170 runs behind. Although there had been one or two heavy showers overnight, there was a strong breeze blowing across the wicket when the West Indies won the toss and began batting on an easy-paced wicket that got faster as the day progressed.

The West Indies showed quite their best form as a batting side, and for the most part played most attractive cricket. G. Challenor was soundness personified and occasionally made some brilliant strokes past cover-point. L.N. Constantine hit vehemently, and one tremendously high on-drive of his cleared the top of the tree just in front of the Buffs' enclosure, probably the biggest hit ever seen on the ground.

C.R. Browne's batting was the feature of the visitors' innings, as he was only at the wicket for just over an hour, and completed a chanceless century and was equally severe on all paces of bowling. His innings was a model of superb strokes, and contained very few careless or reckless strokes, which in so many cases have been the cause of the downfall of the West Indies' batting in big matches. Kent looked to be rather guilty of taking the match in too lighthearted a spirit when fielding, and Freeman appeared tired.

When Kent went in to bat the West Indies' fast bowlers were at their best, although they were not bowling really fast. Both Constantine and H.C. Griffith kept a very good length and got the majority of their wickets by clean bowling the batsmen with splendid balls which did just enough to beat the bat. The majority of the Kent batsmen were guilty of rather overdoing their back play against such bowling.

C.A. Roach and F.R. Martin opened the West Indies' batting against Wright and Ashdown. The first-named was soon caught in the gully in playing too soon at a ball that went away from him. E.L.G. Hoad made a few good strokes on the on side, but fell to a good ball from C.S. Marriott, who appeared to be varying his pace very cleverly. G. Challenor then joined F.R. Martin, who was rather unlucky to be caught from such a brilliant wide left-handed catch by Wright at mid-on from the first big hit which he attempted. R.K. Nunes hit a bad long hop to leg very well, but for the most part was mainly on the defensive, before he was bowled by a very quick breakback.

After the interval M.P. Fernandes was soon out, and Constantine arrived only to be missed from a ridiculously easy catch by Freeman off his own bowling. Once he fell flat in attempting a big hit to square leg off Freeman. His tremendous on-drive over the tree and a straight drive on to the roof of the pavilion were the best hits of a really spectacular display of a quarter of an hour's rather unorthodox batting. G. Challenor, who had played a most correct innings, had another hurricane hitter in C.R. Browne, who directly he arrived began to hit the ball over mid-off's head. He took no undue liberties, but hit the ball with ease and great power, especially when cutting or hitting anything at all short on the leg side. Challenor's fine display ended in his playing a ball hard on to his off stump. Griffith kept up his end while Browne made his last 20 runs that enabled him to complete his splendid century. Although the Kent bowling was never actually mastered, runs were always coming at a great pace. C.S. Marriott and Wright were easily the best of the four regular bowlers....

It was quite one of the best all-round exhibitions of the game that the West Indies have given since their remarkable victory over Middlesex at the beginning of the season.

–The Times,
Monday, August 27, 1928, Page 5

WEST INDIES BIG WIN

In beating Kent at Canterbury yesterday by 201 runs the West Indies team gained the reward of splendid all-round cricket against one of our strongest counties this season. Kent had small hope of averting defeat, for, with seven batsmen out for 98, they still wanted 274 runs to win. J.L. Bryan made a plucky effort, and needed only five runs to complete three figures when the last Kent wicket fell.

After rather more than an hour's play Kent were disposed of for 170, Griffith and Constantine repeating their effective bowling of Monday and sharing the honours. A good deal depended upon Woolley, who, owing to an injured hand, had been unable to bat yesterday, but he was dismissed by a clever running catch by extra cover with 11 runs added to the total. Wright was caught at the wicket at 119, and, of the 72 runs added yesterday, 51 came in the last partnership, when C.S. Marriot played steadily, while J.L. Bryan hit out vigorously.

With Bryan's score at 95 as the result of over two and a half hour's sound batting, Marriott was bowled. Making most of his runs by hard and accurately timed drives, chiefly to the on-side of the wicket, Bryan had as many as fourteen 4's among his figures. Griffith, who in the two innings secured 11 wickets for 118 runs, accomplished his best bowling performance during the tour.

–The Times,
Wednesday, August 29, 1928, Page 6

Appendix

I.—The Game in the West Indies.

Perhaps the earliest association of the game with the West Indies is that provided by George Dehany, who, the only son of George Dehany of Jamaica, played for Old Westminsters, M.C.C., Hampshire, the Gentlemen of England, and Surrey and Sussex combined before the eighteenth century closed. He was too, a member of the Hambledon C.C. Born in 1760, he was called to the Bar in 1784. Thus he flourished many years before Jingle scored 570 in his famous single-wicket match with Sir Thomas Blazo.

The game has probably been played in the West Indies for over 100 years, for as early as 1841-2 the Trinidad C.C. was described as "of very long standing." Of more recent events the following are noteworthy:—

1857-8—Formation of Georgetown C.C., of British Guiana.
1863-3—The Kingston C.C., of Jamaica, established by a few boys on their return from English Public Schools. (King George wired congratulations to the Club on its Jubilee.)
1864-5—The first really big match, Barbados beating British Guiana at Bridgetown by 138 runs.
1883-3—The first 100 in important cricket, E. F. Wright scoring 123 of a total of 168 (including 7 extras) for British Guiana v. Trinidad, at Georgetown.
1886—The first time a West Indian team toured—to United States and Canada.
1887-8—First visit of a side—from United States—from over-seas.
1893-4—First of the regular series of International Tournaments.
1894-5—First visit of an English team—Mr. R. S. Lucas's—to West Indies.
1900—First visit of a West Indian team to England.
1909-10—First Competition—at Queen's Park, Grenada—between Grenada, St. Lucia and St. Vincent for the Cork Cup, presented by the Hon. Philip Clark Cork.
1926-7—Formation—at Bridgetown on January 23, under presidency of L. T. Yearwood—of West Indian Cricket Board of Control. H. B. G. Austin (Barbados) was appointed President for two years, and H. Cole (Barbados) the first Secretary. Barbados, British Guiana, Jamaica and Trinidad have two representatives each, and the Leeward and Windward Islands one each.
1928—Inauguration of Test-matches between England and West Indies.

West Indian Teams on Tour.

	Won	Lost	Drn.	Total
1886—In United States and Canada	6	5	2	13
1900—In England	5	8	4	17
1906—In England	7	10	2	19
1923—In England	13	7	8	28

Attempts to arrange visits to England in 1888 and 1889 were unsuccessful.

Teams on Tour in the West Indies.

	Won	Lost	Drn.	Total
1887-8—United States Team	5	4	2	11
1894-5—R. S. Lucas's	10	4	2	16
1896-7—Lord Hawke's	9	2	3	14
1901-2—A. Priestley's	10	5	1	16
1904-5—R. A. Bennett's	13	3	3	19
1908-9—Lord Brackley's	12	3	5	20
1910-1—Philadelphians†	4	1	1	6
1912-3—M.C.C.'s	4	4	4*	12
1913-3—M.C.C.'s	5	3	1	9
1926-6—M.C.C.'s	2	1	10	13
1926-7—L. H. Tennyson's†	1	0	6	7
1927-8—L. H. Tennyson's†	1	2	2	5

† Played in Jamaica only.   * Includes a tie.

A proposed visit of a Canadian team in September, 1889, fell through.

Tournament Winners.

Since the first of the Competitions in the recognised series took place, the winners have been:—

1893-4—Barbados	1909-0—Trinidad
1895-6—British Guiana	1910-1—Barbados
1897-8—Barbardos	1911-2—,"
1899-0—,"	1921-2—Unfinished
1901-2—Trinidad	1922-3—Barbados
1903-4—,"	1923-4—,"
1905-6—Barbados	1924-5—Trinidad
1907-8—Trinidad	1925-6—,"
1908-9—Barbados	1926-7—Barbados

The Tournaments have taken place at Port of Spain, Georgetown, and Kensington (Barbados) in turn.

Harlequins v West Indies
The Saffrons, Eastbourne - 29, 30, 31 August, 1928 (3-day match)

Result: Harlequins won by an innings & 105 runs
Umpires: J Moss and WAJ West

West Indies 1st innings
CA Roach	lbw	b Robertson-Glasgow	3
FR Martin	c Lowndes	b Robertson-Glasgow	8
ELG Hoad	run out		34
EA Rae	c Lowndes	b Robertson-Glasgow	0
EL Bartlett		b Holmes	5
*CV Wight	lbw	b Evans	10
CR Browne		b Holmes	60
JA Small	not out		98
JM Neblett		b Bettington	17
HC Griffith		b Holmes	1
GN Francis	c Lowndes	b Burton	61
Extras	(b 9, lb 5)		14
Total	**(all out, 72 overs)**		**311**

Holmes 22-1-77-3   Evans 4-1-18-1   Robertson-Glasgow 19-3-80-3
Bettington 13-0-61-1   Stevens 2-0-4-0   Lowndes 2-0-12-0
Franklin 3-1-14-0   Burton 4-0-19-1   Garland-Wells 3-0-12-0

Harlequins 1st innings
RC Burton		b Francis	52
GTS Stevens		b Griffith	21
WGLF Lowndes		b Griffith	10
ERT Holmes		b Francis	3
CH Knott	not out		261
HM Garland-Wells		b Griffith	35
RHB Bettington	c Wight	b Neblett	127
AJ Evans	c Roach	b Small	124
HWF Franklin		b Small	11
Extras	(b 21, lb 8, nb 3)		32
Total	**(8 wickets declared, 141.5 overs)**		**676**

DNB: +FW Gilligan, RC Robertson-Glasgow.

Francis 27-2-103-2   Griffith 33-2-154-3   Browne 35-2-128-0
Small 17.5-1-70-2   Martin 5-0-14-0   Neblett 13-3-71-1
Hoad 9-0-81-0   Rae 2-0-23-0

West Indies 2nd innings
CA Roach		b Robertson-Glasgow	12
FR Martin	c Gilligan	b Robertson-Glasgow	0
ELG Hoad		b Holmes	21
EA Rae	c Holmes	b Burton	42
EL Bartlett	st Gilligan	b Garland-Wells	47
*CV Wight	lbw	b Bettington	8
CR Browne	run out		16
JA Small		b Robertson-Glasgow	5
JM Neblett		b Bettington	21
HC Griffith		b Bettington	48
GN Francis	not out		32
Extras	(b 1, lb 6, w 1)		8
Total	**(all out, 67.2 overs)**		**260**

Holmes 17-3-61-1   Stevens 14-2-45-0   Bettington 10.2-2-62-3
Burton 6-1-23-1   Knott 2-0-16-0   Garland-Wells 2-0-7-1
Robertson-Glasgow 16-4-38-3

Appendix

II.—The West Indies Team.

Of the 17 players Barbados has supplied 5, and Trinidad, British Guiana and Jamaica 4 apiece. (Barbados is little more than half the size of the Isle of Wight, Trinidad is slightly larger than Somerset, the British Guiana men belong to Georgetown, and Jamaica, the biggest island in the British West Indies, is about three-quarters the size of Yorkshire.)

The selection was made by L. T. Yearwood (Barbados), J. G. Kelshall (Trinidad), C. Shankland (British Guiana) and Major G. S. Cox, M.C. (Jamaica), with H. B. G. Austin, President of the West Indies Cricket Board of Control, in the chair. The colours adopted are deep burgundy blazer with West Indian crest on breast pocket, with tie, sash, &c., of same colour background with a quarter inch stripes of green and silver.

The cricketers touring are:

Bartlett, E. L. (Barbados). Useful bat. In the Tournament of 1926-7 made 88 v. British Guiana and 17 and 74 v. Trinidad, adding 216 for 8th wicket in former game with C. A. Browne. Scored 93* for Barbados-Born v. Rest of West Indies in January. Born March 18, 1906.

Browne, C. R. (British Guiana). Played formerly for Barbados. An attractive bat and good right-hand, medium-paced bowler. During tour of 1923 took 96 wickets for 20 runs each—7 for 97 v. Notts. For British Guiana v. Barbados, 1925-6, scored 102 and took 13 for 135, and same season made 103* for West Indies v. M.C.C. at Georgetown. Before the War, whilst studying Law, played club cricket in England. Born Oct. 8, 1890.

Challenor, G. (Barbados). The best bat yet produced by West Indies, and can also bowl a useful ball. Came over with the team of 1906—1,017 runs (aver. 29·05), 108 v. Notts.—and 1923 (1,967 runs (aver. 50·43),

making eight 100s. For Barbados has scored 118, 109, and 124 v. M.C.C. 104, 114, and 220 v. Trinidad, 237* v. Jamaica, and 104 v. British Guiana. Had made many long stands for first wicket with P. H. Tarilton, including 292 v. Trinidad in 1926-7 and 219* v. Notts. in 1923. Played twice for Wanderers v. Pickwick in 1920-1, scoring 261 in first match and 206 and 133 in second. Born June 28, 1888.

Constantine, L. S., jun. (Trinidad). Splendid field, especially at cover, a free-hitting bat and useful bowler. His father toured here in 1900 and 1906, and he himself in 1923. Took 8 for 38 for Trinidad v. Barbados, 1923-4, and during his 1923 tour 51 for 18¼ runs each. Born Sept. 21, 1902.

Fernandes, M. P. (British Guiana). A capital bat, but owes his place to the withdrawal of G. A. Dewhurst, the wicket-keeper. Came over in 1923, when ill-health handicapped him, though he was second in the side's first-class averages. Made 110 v. Leicestershire, and 49 and 73 v. Lancashire at Manchester, in latter game adding over 100—131 and 102—for fifth wicket with Small in each innings. In 1926-5 scored 124 v. Trinidad and 120 v. M.C.C., in each case for British Guiana at Georgetown. For some years captained the Demerara C.C., and has led British Guiana also. Born Aug. 12, 1897.

Francis, G. (Barbados). Fast bowler with good command over ball. Toured here in 1923, taking 102 wickets for 15·34—3 in 4 balls v. Surrey, 4 for 12 v. H. D. G. Leveson-Gower's XI. at Scarborough. In former game also made 41, adding 136 for last wicket with Challenor. Had 7 for 50 for Barbados v. M.C.C. 1925-6. Born Dec. 7, 1897.

Griffith, M. C. (Barbados). Bowls fast-medium—fast through air and off pitch. For Barbados took 7 for 38 v. Trinidad in 1921-2, 10 for 78 v. same side in 1923-4, and 5 for 54 and 4 for 42 in 1925-6 v. M.C.C., who were beaten by an innings. Born Dec. 1, 1893.

THE 1928 ARCHIVES

HARLEQUINS v. WEST INDIES
A LAST-WICKET STAND

In the match between the Harlequins and the West Indies, which was begun at Eastbourne yesterday, the West Indies, after a poor start, scored 311, Small and Francis making a fine stand for the last wicket. The Harlequins had scored 152 for the loss of four wickets before close of play.

Years ago, when the number of first-class counties was less by nearly 50 per cent than it is now, the Australians used to fill vacant dates in their programme by playing the Harlequins or the Quidnuncs as "Oxford or Cambridge, Past and Present." Twice at least the two University clubs combined forces, and on one of these occasions the Australians set up a record by scoring 843 in their one innings. Arguments could be adduced to show that since those far-off days the standard of University cricket has improved relatively to that reached in the competition for the County Championship. Then a man who had played for his county before going up to Oxford or Cambridge assumed a Blue almost as a matter of course. Now it occasions no surprise if a man who has failed to get a place in the University match at Lord's plays regularly for his county during the Long Vacation. Of Blues even those who were decorated for their bowling are invited by the secretaries of the county clubs, excepting two or three of the strongest, to name the dates when they can assist. Therefore the West Indies, however uplifted they may have been by their smashing victory over Kent, at Canterbury of all places, would not have been justified in proceeding to Eastbourne with the idea that they were going to enjoy three days of picnic cricket.

Cricket is an extraordinarily good game to watch when something is happening all the time. Yesterday's play fairly bristled with interest. The West Indies left out three of their best players, Nunes, Challenor, and Constantine, and, when they had lost six wickets for 64, seemed in a fair way to pay for their temerity. Chief cause of the early disasters was the admirable bowling of Robertson-Glasgow, who made the ball do all manner of strange things in the air and whip off the ground unpleasantly fast. The gestures of the batsmen and of Gilligan, the highly competent wicket-keeper, showed how difficult he was. Nevertheless, the batsmen persisted in going for their strokes. It must be admitted that they were not conspicuously discreet in selecting the strokes

George Challenor.
The West Indies left him, Constantine and Nurse out of this game.

to go for. Two tried to hit straight balls to leg and were out leg-before-wicket. Martin slashed at an off-ball and was nicely caught in the slips. Bartlett, the third man to hit across a straight ball, was bowled. Then Hoad and Browne, batting very well, improved matters, but Hoad ran himself out at 64 and Rae was immediately caught in the slips.

At the crisis Browne and Small played confident and brilliant cricket. In little more than an hour they put on exactly 100 runs. Evans could neither find the bowler nor place the field for them. They had pulled the game round when, in the last over before luncheon, Browne hit across a straight half-volley. The cheap dismissal of Small is clearly one of Oxford's lost causes. He got 100 at Oxford, and yesterday took out his bat for 98. Neblett, the left-hander, kept up his wicket for a time manfully, and himself made a series of good strikes behind the wicket on the off side. Finally Francis batted in a manner quite indecent for one who comes in next before the roller. He hit hard and freely without using the fast bowler's slog. The last wicket put on 107 runs, all of them good, in little more than an hour, and the total reached 311, which represents a fine performance by a side which was once in danger of collapsing. It was achieved against a team whose captain used nine bowlers, G.T.S. Stevens the ninth.

Stevens and the Old Malvernian, Burton, opened the batting for the Harlequins. Both played the fast bowling of Griffith and Francis comfortably and placed their strokes so well that runs came fast. It was surprising as well as disappointing when Stevens missed a ball pitched well up to him and was bowled. Lowndes also seemed at home from the first ball he received and cut delightfully. But he early took a liberty with a straight long hop and missed it. Holmes never timed the ball so accurately as his predecessors, and was soon bowled. Shortly afterwards Francis uncaged a terrific break back to beat Burton, who had played an absolutely first-class innings with every stroke in the game finely executed. He is qualified for Sussex. Subsequently Knott and Garland-Wells contributed materially to a day's display which would have satisfied the most earnest pleader for brighter cricket.

–The Times,
Thursday, August 30, 1928, Page 6

Appendix

Hoad, E. L. G. (Barbados). Good but with sound defence, though can score fast, and bowls useful slows. For Barbados made 160* v. Jamaica in 1924-5, and 115 v. British Guiana, 174* v. Trinidad, and 123* v. Leeward Islands, all in 1926-7. In last-mentioned game adding 209 for second wicket with L. S. Birkett. In January last, in the third Trial match, he scored 153 for Barbados-Born v. Rest of West Indies, he and Tarilton putting-on 288 for second match. Took 8 for 33 v. Antigua in 1926-7. Born Jan. 29, 1896.

Martin, F. R. (Jamaica). Skilful left-handed bat, and can bowl a useful ball. In his first big game scored 195 (run out) for Jamaica v. Barbados in 1924-5. Two seasons later made 204* for same side v. L. H. Tennyson's Team. Born Oct. 12, 1893.

Neblett, J. (British Guiana). Bowls left-hand slow-medium with good action, varying pace and break cleverly. Can bat, too, and in one recent Trial game scored 59 whilst only 5 other runs were being made from the bat. Born Nov. 13, 1901.

Nunes, R. K. (Jamaica). Captain of side. Very good left-handed bat and can keep wicket well. Was in the Dulwich College XI. in 1910, 1911 (aver. 59-23), and 1912 (aver. 40½), and has played for Surrey 2nd. (60* v. Cheshire, 1919). Was Vice-Captain of team which came over in 1923, when he was not seen at his best. For Jamaica has made 140* v. M.C.C. in 1925-6, and—in separate games—200* and 108 v. L. H. Tennyson's Team in 1926-7. Born June 7, 1894.

Rae, E. A. (Jamaica). A hard-hitting bat, safe long-field, and change bowler (leg-breaks). In making 98 and 84, in different matches, for Jamaica v. L. H. Tennyson's Team in 1926-7, he took part in stands of 179 for the sixth wicket and 178 for the fourth. Last January scored 80, in a Trial-match, for Rest of West Indies v. Barbados-Born. In July, 1921, made 152 in 65 minutes for Kingston, hitting nine 6s. Born Nov. 8, 1897.

Roach, C. (Trinidad). Useful bat, fair change bowler, and excellent field. For Trinidad made 44 and 22 v. British Guiana in 1923-4, and 32 v. M.C.C. in 1925-6. Last December, in the First Trial game, he scored 54 for Trinidad and British Guiana v. Jamaica and Barbados, adding 159 for second wicket with W. St. Hill. Born March 13, 1904.

St. Hill, W. (Trinidad). An entertaining, free-hitting bat. For Trinidad has made 104 v. British Guiana in 1921-2, and 100 v. same side and 105 v. M.C.C., both in 1925-6. Also 95 v. Barbados in 1919-20. In the first of the recent Trial-matches he scored 144, hitting 25 fours, for Trinidad and British Guiana v. Jamaica and Barbados. In the third Trial he made 44 and 71. Born July 6, 1893.

Scott, O. C. (Jamaica). Now almost a veteran, but a good all-rounder, and possibly West Indies' best slow bowler. Took 11 for 138 in a game for Jamaica v. M.C.C. in 1910-11, and in three matches between the same sides in 1925-6 scored 14 and 54, 58 and 72, 62. Early this year in two successive games v. Tennyson's Team took 4 for 81, 6 for 75, 4 for 65, and 8 for 67 (in total of 259) besides making 69 runs in three innings. The last player chosen and a popular choice. Born Aug. 25, 1893.

Small, J. A. (Trinidad). Attractive bat and good medium-fast bowler. For the team of 1923 he made 1,169 runs (aver. 32·47) (131 v. Wilts.), and bowled well on occasion—6 for 18 v. Cheshire. For Trinidad has scored 102* v. Barbados in 1919-20, 133 v. British Guiana in 1925-6, and 100 v. Barbados in 1926-7. Against Lancashire in 1923 he made 94 and 68. Took 7 for 49 for Trinidad v. M.C.C. in 1912-13, and 3 for 8 in the first of the recent Trial games. Born Nov. 3, 1892.

Wight, C. V. (British Guiana). Vice-Captain of side. An attractive and stylish bat and an excellent field. For West Indies v. M.C.C. at Georgetown, 1925-6, made 90, adding 173 for seventh wicket with C. R. Browne. Last January scored 119* for Rest of West Indies v. Barbados-Born. Born July 28, 1902.

* Signifies not out.

England XI v West Indies
Municipal Ground, Folkestone - 1, 3, 4 September, 1928 (3-day match)

Result: England XI won by 4 wickets
Umpires: F Chester and J Stone

West Indies 1st innings
CA Roach	run out		30
FR Martin	c Ames	b Hammond	46
MP Fernandes	lbw	b Freeman	11
G Challenor	c Woolley	b Hammond	38
JA Small	c Ames	b Freeman	1
EL Bartlett		b Robins	25
LN Constantine	lbw	b Freeman	7
CR Browne		b Freeman	17
*+RK Nunes	c Woolley	b Freeman	6
GN Francis		b Freeman	5
HC Griffith	not out		4
Extras	(b 3, lb 19)		22
Total	**(all out, 73 overs)**		**212**

Hammond 17-5-41-2 Calthorpe 6-2-8-0 Freeman 29-2-87-6
Wyatt 9-3-26-0 Robins 12-2-28-1

England XI 1st innings
HW Lee		b Constantine	14
RES Wyatt	c Fernandes	b Constantine	42
FE Woolley	c Small	b Griffith	33
WR Hammond	lbw	b Constantine	32
+LEG Ames	c Constantine	b Small	42
*LH Tennyson	c Martin	b Constantine	0
HM Garland-Wells		b Griffith	6
RWV Robins	run out		2
FT Mann	c Fernandes	b Small	6
FSG Calthorpe	c Griffith	b Small	4
AP Freeman	not out		1
Extras	(b 8, lb 5, nb 3)		16
Total	**(all out, 53.3 overs)**		**198**

Francis 12-3-19-0 Griffith 17-0-78-2 Constantine 20-2-66-4
Small 4.3-1-19-3

West Indies 2nd innings
CA Roach	lbw	b Garland-Wells	60
FR Martin		b Freeman	38
MP Fernandes	run out		15
G Challenor	lbw	b Freeman	13
JA Small	c Robins	b Freeman	7
EL Bartlett	c Hammond	b Robins	8
LN Constantine		b Hammond	62
CR Browne		b Hammond	28
*+RK Nunes		b Freeman	4
GN Francis	not out		15
HC Griffith	st Ames	b Freeman	1
Extras	(b 11, lb 8, nb 1)		20
Total	**(all out, 81.3 overs)**		**271**

Hammond 12-1-44-2 Calthorpe 4-2-4-0 Freeman 29.3-4-109-5
Wyatt 8-2-17-0 Robins 24-8-73-1 Garland-Wells 4-2-4-1

England XI 2nd innings (target: 286 runs)
HW Lee	run out		1
RES Wyatt	c Constantine	b Griffith	75
FE Woolley	hit wicket	b Francis	151
WR Hammond		b Griffith	4
+LEG Ames	c Challenor	b Small	13
*LH Tennyson	c Small	b Constantine	8
HM Garland-Wells	not out		18
RWV Robins	not out		4
Extras	(b 7, lb 3, nb 4)		14
Total	**(6 wickets, 52 overs)**		**288**

DNB: FT Mann, FSG Calthorpe, AP Freeman.

Francis 12-1-45-1 Griffith 12-1-81-2 Constantine 17-1-91-1
Small 6-0-40-1 Browne 5-0-17-0

III.—Anglo-West Indian Records.

BATTING.

Largest Individual Scores.

(a)—For English Sides:

244, Holmes, P., M.C.C. v. Jamaica, 1925-6
238*, Hammond, M.C.C. v. West Indies, at Kensington, 1925-6
182, Stevens, G. T. S., Oxford Univ. v. West Indies, 1923
173, Hayes, Lord Brackley's Team v. St. Lucia, 1904-5

(b)—For West Indian Sides:

211, Headley, G., Jamaica v. L. H. Tennyson's Team, 1927-8
204*, Martin, F. R., Jamaica v. L. H. Tennyson's Team, 1926-7
200*, Nunes, R. K., Jamaica v. L. H. Tennyson's Team, 1926-7
178, Tarilton, P. H., Barbados v. M.C.C., 1925-6
159 v. Leicestershire, in 1900

NOTE: The highest in England is C. A. Ollivierre's 159 v. Leicestershire, in 1900

Record Partnerships.

Wkt. *(a)—For English Sides:*

1st —230, B. H. Holloway (100) and T. A. L. Whittington (154), M.C.C. v. British Guiana, 1910-11
2nd—211, Makepeace (111) and Tyldesley (E.) (105), for Lancashire, 1923
3rd—203, O'Connor (103) and Tyldesley (E.) (106), L. H. Tennyson's v. XVI. Jamaica Colts, 1926-7
4th—196, J. L. Guise (120) and G. T. S. Stevens (182), for Oxford University, 1923
5th—327, Astill (156) and Holmes (244), M.C.C. v. Jamaica, 1926-6

6th—218, Hammond (238*) and T. O. Jameson (98), M.C.C. v. West Indies, at Kensington, 1925-6
7th—154, H. R. Bromley-Davenport (91) and J. M. Dawson (138), R. S. Lucas' v. Barbados, 1894-5
8th—130, Astill (66) and Hammond (238*), M.C.C. v. West Indies, at Kensington, 1925-6
9th—168, L. G. Crawley (85) and Watson (103*), M.C.C. v. Jamaica, 1925-6
10th—167, Smith, W. C. (126) and A. W. F. Somerset (55*), M.C.C. v. Barbados, 1912-13

NOTE: In an XI. a-side game for the third wicket—187, Gunn, W., and Iremonger, for Notts, 1900

(b)—For West Indian Sides:

Wkt.
1st —238, C. A. Ollivierre (159) and P. F. Warner (113), v. Leicestershire, 1900
2nd—215, G. Headley (211) and C. M. Morales (84), Jamaica v. L. H. Tennysons, 1927-8
3rd—141, G. Challenor (101) and H. W. Ince (60), v. Norfolk, 1923
4th—178, F. R. Martin (204*) and E. A. Rae (84), Jamaica v. L. H. Tennyson's Team, 1926-7
5th—136, W. E. Goodman (65) and S. W. Sproston (95), British Guiana v. Lord Hawke's Team, 1896-7
6th—179, R. K. Nunes (200*) and E. A. Rae (98), Jamaica v. L. H. Tennyson's Team, 1926-7
7th—173, C. R. Browne (102*) and C. V. Wight (90), West Indies v. M.C.C., at Georgetown, 1925-6
8th—123, C. A. Browne (61) and P. H. Tarilton (157), Barbados v. M.C.C., 1912-13
9th—162, Burton (64*) and L. S. Constantine (113), v. M.C.C., at Lord's, 1900
10th—136, G. Challenor (155*) and Francis (41) v. Surrey, 1923
11th—108* D. Beckford (36*) and H. F. Bicknell (76*), XVI. Jamaica Colts v. L. H. Tennyson's Team, 1926-7

THE 1928 ARCHIVES

WEST INDIES AT FOLKESTONE
GOOD BOWLING BY FREEMAN

The first match of the annual Folkestone festival, between the West Indies and an England Eleven, began on Saturday in glorious weather. The wicket was fast and perfect and the light almost tropical in its brilliance, conditions which should have suited our visitors to perfection, but they had considerably the worst of the play. After completing an innings for 212, they were able to dismiss two of their opponents only for 114.

The wicket in use at Folkestone this year for important matches is considerably

Learie Constantine

nearer the pavilion than it was in previous years, a great improvement from the point of view of the spectators, for the game, which used to be decidedly remote, has become quite intimate.

The West Indies started with C.A. Roach and F.R. Martin to the bowling of Hammond and F.S.G. Calthorpe. For a time runs came very slowly and it was nearly half an hour before the first boundary hit was made, a square-leg shot by Roach off Hammond. Once started, however, Roach began to bat very freely, driving Calthorpe to the boundary and Hammond to the pavilion rails. This caused a double change of bowling, Freeman for Hammond, and R.E.S. Wyatt for Calthorpe, but Roach hit each bowler for 4 before being out rather unluckily. Martin hit a ball wide of R.W.V. Robins at short-leg, and it looked a safe run, but Robins gathered the ball at the extremity of his reach and threw down the wicket before Roach could get home.

With M.P. Fernandes in the 50 went up in an hour, in spite of the very slow start, but directly afterwards he was leg-before to Freeman. G. Challenor and Martin increased the rate of scoring, though the former was missed at slip by Woolley when he had made 17, and, in spite of bowling changes, the pair were together at luncheon time, when the score was 107, after an hour and 40 minutes' play.

The visitors had a disastrous hour after luncheon. With 17 runs added Woolley atoned for his previous error by catching Challenor in the slips, and one run later J.A. Small was caught at the wicket. E.L. Bartlett and Martin, who was batting with much greater freedom, added runs quickly, but the latter, just as he neared is 50, was well caught at the wicket wide on the off side, and half the side was out for 146. His patient batting – he was in for two hours and a quarter – was of great value to his side. L.N. Constantine, who followed, made a short, but eventful, appearance. He hit the first ball to leg for 2, and was nearly run out by a good return of Robins, and that fieldsman missed him, a very difficult chance, off the next ball. When facing Freeman he drove him to the off boundary, a glorious stroke, and was out next ball, leg-before-wicket, in trying to hook him to leg. Bartlett and C.R. Browne improved matters and raised the score to 184, when the latter was bowled by Freeman with a ball which looked to turn a foot. After that the end soon came, in spite of some plucky batting by Bartlett. G.N. Francis was bowled round his legs by Freeman, and R.K. Nunes gave Woolley the easiest of catches off the same bowler, and the side was out at 4 o'clock for 212. Once again the visitors showed their dislike of good slow bowling, and Freeman's figures of six for 87 were impressive. He was tossing his slows up into the wind very cleverly, and keeping an irreproachable length. R.E.S. Wyatt and Lee had some very good bowling to face from Constantine and Francis when the England eleven went into bat, and for a time runs came very slowly, but it was not till Constantine changed ends that a wicket fell, Lee playing a ball from him hard on to his wicket. This was at 41, and in the following over Wyatt opened his shoulders to Griffith, and hit him to the boundary off four successive balls, the last two strokes being made almost off the batsman's eyebrow. After his dismissal, caught at the wicket, Hammond and Woolley played sound cricket, but the bowling was too good to take liberties with, and the fielding exceptionally good.

–*The Times*,
Monday, September 3, 1928, Page 5

Appendix

Carrying Bat Through Completed Innings.

(a).—*For English Sides*:
126, Dipper, for Gloucestershire, 1923
115, Whittington, T. A. L., M.C.C. v. Jamaica, 1910-11

(b).—*For West Indian Sides*:
155, Challenor, G. v. Surrey, 1923
47, Challenor, G. v. Durham, 1923
104, Moulder, E. R. D., West Indies v. M.C.C. at Georgetown, 1912-13
32, North, M. K., British Guiana v. R. S. Lucas's Team, 1894-5
200, Nunes, R. K., Jamaica v. L. H. Tennyson's Team, 1926-7

1,000 or more Runs during Tour.

(a).—*For English Sides*:

	Inn.	NotOut.	Most.	Total.	Average
1896-7 Stoddart, A. E.	23	3	153*	1,079	53.95

(b).—*For West Indian Sides*:

	Inn.	NotOut.	Most.	Total.	Average
1906 Challenor, G.	35	0	108	1,017	29.05
1923 " "	46	7	155*	1,907	50.43
1906 Constantine, L. S.	35	0	92	1,025	29.28
1923 Small, J. A.	41	5	131	1,169	32.47
1906 Smith, S. G.	37	4	140*	1,107	33.54

Fast Scoring.

(a).—*For English Sides*:

G. L. Jessop made 157 out of 201 in hour for Gloucestershire, 1900, hitting 29 fours, five of them in an over. At one time, whilst in with C. L. Townsend, he scored 83 out of 105 in half-hour

Hayes made 173 in 2 hours, hitting ten 6s, for Lord Brackley's Team v. St. Lucia, 1904-5

(b).—*For West Indian Sides*:

T. Osment scored 82 in half-hour, hitting five 6s and eight 4s, for St Vincent v. Lord Brackley's Team, 1904-5

Varia.

(a).—*For English Sides*:

A. E. Stoddart made 143 of total of 237 (25 extras) for A. Priestley's Team v. Jamaica, 1896-7. Next highest score was only 18

C. L. Townsend, in making 140 for Gloucestershire, 1900, added 209 for 5th wicket with Wrathall (123) and 201 for 6th with G. L. Jessop (157)

V. F. S. Crawford, for Leicestershire, 1906, hit five 4s off an over from C. A. Ollivierre

Smith, W. C., going in last for M.C.C. v. Barbados, 1912-13, made 126 out of 167 in 1¼ hours

Hammond, in making 238* for M.C.C. v. West Indies, at Kensington, 1925-6, added 131 for 3rd wicket with Smith (E. J.) (79), 218 for 6th with T. O. Jameson (96), and 130 for 8th with Astill (66)

T. Arnott hit six 6s, and seven 4s in making 71 in 50 minutes for L. H. Tennyson's Team v. Jamaica, 1926-7

(b).—*For West Indian Sides*:

Martin, H. A., batted 2 hours for 23 runs for St. George's C.C. v. Lord Hawke's Team, at Grenada, 1896-7
Sproston, S. W. (118), for West Indies v. Liverpool and District, 1900, made 54 whilst the last man in scored 1*

Constantine, L. S., claimed 60 of the last 69 made from the bat in 75 minutes by the last 4 wickets v. W. G. Grace's XI., at the Crystal Palace, 1906

HDG Leveson-Gower's XI v West Indies

North Marine Road Ground, Scarborough - 8, 10, 11 Sept, 1928 (3-day match)

Result: HDG Leveson-Gower's XI won by 8 wickets
Umpires: D Denton and GH Hirst

West Indies 1st innings

CA Roach	c Gilligan	b Tate	13
FR Martin	lbw	b Robinson	6
ELG Hoad	run out		124
*+RK Nunes	lbw	b Tate	1
G Challenor		b Haig	5
EL Bartlett	lbw	b Jupp	28
LN Constantine		b Robinson	50
CR Browne	c Sutcliffe	b Tate	34
JA Small	lbw	b Wyatt	20
GN Francis	c Hobbs	b Haig	12
HC Griffith	not out		24
Extras	(b 10, lb 5, w 1)		16
Total	**(all out, 76.4 overs)**		**333**

Tate 18.4-1-80-3 Robinson 14-1-59-2 Haig 19-1-53-2
Jupp 15-1-84-1 Wyatt 10-0-41-1

HDG Leveson-Gower's XI 1st innings

JB Hobbs	lbw	b Constantine	14
H Sutcliffe		b Constantine	64
A Sandham	c Constantine	b Francis	5
KS Duleepsinhji	lbw	b Constantine	34
RES Wyatt	c Browne	b Small	19
E Robinson	c Constantine	b Francis	15
NE Haig	c Roach	b Constantine	31
VWC Jupp		b Constantine	3
MW Tate	lbw	b Constantine	0
JWHT Douglas	not out		27
+FW Gilligan	c Francis	b Constantine	14
Extras	(b 2, lb 5, w 2, nb1)		10
Total	**(all out, 96.5 overs)**		**236**

Francis 29-9-68-2 Constantine 24.5-7-68-7 Griffith 19-2-49-0
Browne 10-2-26-0 Small 14-8-15-1

West Indies 2nd innings

CA Roach	c Gilligan	b Tate	1
FR Martin	c Gilligan	b Tate	40
ELG Hoad		b Tate	30
*+RK Nunes		b Tate	8
G Challenor		b Jupp	5
EL Bartlett		b Haig	3
LN Constantine	c Duleepsinhji	b Jupp	11
CR Browne	c Haig	b Jupp	1
JA Small	c Gilligan	b Jupp	0
GN Francis		b Tate	4
HC Griffith	not out		7
Extras	(b 1, lb 2)		3
Total	**(all out, 49.3 overs)**		**113**

Tate 21.3-5-28-5 Robinson 13-2-22-0 Haig 8-1-27-1
Jupp 7-0-33-4

HDG Leveson-Gower's XI 2nd innings (target: 211 runs)

JB Hobbs	not out		119
H Sutcliffe	c Nunes	b Browne	37
A Sandham	c Martin	b Francis	27
KS Duleepsinhji	not out		27
Extras	(b 1, lb 1)		2
Total	**(2 wickets, 39.4 overs)**		**212**

DNB: RES Wyatt, E Robinson, NE Haig, VWC Jupp, MW Tate, JWHT Douglas, +FW Gilligan.

Francis 11.4-1-62-1 Griffith 5-1-23-0 Constantine 12-1-66-0
Browne 8-0-47-1 Small 3-0-12-0

Appendix

14

Harragin, A. E., made 50 out of 76 in 25 mins, by means of five 6s, four 4s and two 2s, v. W. G. Grace's XI., at the Crystal Palace, 1906

Constantine, L. S., v. Yorkshire, at Harrogate, 1906, hit five 4s off an over from Sedgwick

Tarilton, P. H., in making 157 for Barbados v. M.C.C. in 1912-13, added 134 for 7th wicket with G. Challenor (109), 128 for 8th with C. A. Browne (61), and 100 for 10th with H. W. Ince (57*)

Constantine, L. S., jun., in 1923, scored 60* out of 74 in 45 minutes v. Derbyshire, and 23 in 7 minutes v. Gloucestershire.

Challenor, G. (63) took 2¼ hours to make his last 26 for West Indies v. M.C.C, at Kensington, 1925-6

Tarilton, P. H., in scoring 178 for Barbados, v. M.C.C. in 1925-6, added 146 for 2nd wicket with E. L. G. Hoad (71), 100 for 3rd with H. W. Ince (87), and 99 for 4th with L. S. Birkett (52*)

* Signifies not out.

BOWLING.

Most Wickets in an Innings.

(a)—*For English Sides*:

10 for 38, Dowson, E. M., R. A. Bennett's Team v. 16 Jamaica Colts, 1901-2

9 for 41, Bromley-Davenport H. R., R. S. Lucas's Team v. St. Lucia 12, 1894-5

9 for 22, Bush, F. W., R. S. Lucas's Team v. Queen's Park 12, at Port of Spain, 1894-5

9 for 49, Thompson, Lord Brackley's Team v. Queen's Park, at Port of Spain, 1904-5

9 for 44, Vogler, M.C.C. v. West Indies, at Lord's, 1906

9 for 49, Hilder, A. L., L. H. Tennyson's Team v. 15 Middlesex, at Port Maria, 1927-8

15

(b)—*For West Indian Sides*:

9 for 79, Ollivierre, R. A., Grenada and St. Vincent v. R. A. Bennett's Team, 1901-2

9 for 34, Smith, S. G., West Indies v. R. A. Bennett's Team, at Port of Spain, 1901-2

Most Wickets in a Match.

(a)—*For English Sides*:

16 for 58, Dowson, E. M., R. A. Bennett's Team v. Jamaica, 1901-2

16 for 70, Thompson, Lord Brackley's Team v. Queen's Park, at Port of Spain, 1904-5

NOTE: In England the record is 13 for 187 by Llewellyn for Hampshire, in 1900

(b)—*For West Indian Sides*:

16 for 85, Smith, S. G., West Indies v. R. A. Bennett's Team, at Port of Spain, 1901-2

NOTE: In England the record is 14 for 100 by John for West Indies v. Lord Harris's XI., 1923

Some Noteworthy Figures.

(a)—*For English Sides*:

13 for 39, Bromley-Davenport, H. R., R. S. Lucas's Team v. British Guiana, 1894-5. (Includes 7 for 17)

10 for 22, Bromley-Davenport, H. R., R. S. Lucas's Team v. St. Kitts, 1894-5. (Includes 6 for 3)

9 for 22, Bush, F. W., R. S. Lucas's Team v. Queen's Park 12, at Port of Spain, 1894-5

8 for 18, Burn, R. C. W., Lord Brackley's Team v. Jamaica 18, 1904-5

7 for 16, Wilson, E. R., A. R. Bennett's Team v. West Indies, at Georgetown, 1901-2

NOTE: In England, 5 for 14 by A. E. R. Gilligan for Sussex, 1923

THE 1928 ARCHIVES

WEST INDIES DO WELL AT SCARBOROUGH

The West Indies, in their match with Mr. H.D.G. Leveson-Gower's XI at Scarborough, did very well yesterday to obtain a lead of 97 runs on the first innings. Going in again, they scored 22 runs for one wicket in the last 30 minutes, and so finished up 119 runs ahead with nine wickets in hand.

L.N. Constantine took seven wickets, and his fast bowling, combined with the electrifying agility of his fielding, completely captured the imagination of the crowd. The West Indies out-cricket, however, did not depend for its excellence on Constantine alone. R.K. Nunes kept wicket and managed his bowling splendidly, and the fielding, apart from two dropped slip catches, blemishes one has learnt to regard as inevitable when the West Indies are in the field, was keen enough to make the batsmen almost excessively cautious in their running between the wickets.

The weather was again beautifully fine yesterday morning when Sutcliffe and K.S. Duleepsinhji continued Mr. Leveson-Gower's team innings. Sutcliffe had not been altogether happy on the Saturday evening, and H.C. Griffith, who, bringing the ball back sharply, bowled extremely well, and Constantine soon gave him again the opportunity to show that courage and determination in the face of adversity that is perhaps the most admirable thing about his cricket. Griffith injured him in both the physical and moral sense of the word, but, paradoxical as it may seem, the more he was beaten the more probable a big score from him became. K.S. Duleepsinhji, who has had a splendid festival, caught him up quickly and passed him, but at 84 he was l-b-w to a ball of Constantine's he tried to pull. Before this he had been missed in the slips by C.R. Browne. Sutcliffe and R.E.S. Wyatt then added 50 careful runs. Sutcliffe, at last timing the ball as he wished, glanced Griffith to the fine leg boundary to bring up the hundred, and in the same over he hit him square for another 4. Soon afterwards he again got two 4's to one over off Griffith, the first a stroke through the covers that only he could have made, and the second a pull that gave him his 50. At 134 Wyatt was very easily caught by Browne at first slip off J.A. Small, but Robinson stayed with Sutcliffe until luncheon, when the score was 142 – of which Sutcliffe had made 50 and Robinson three – for four wickets.

Afterwards the initiative very definitely passed from the batsmen to the bowlers and the Scarborough crowd saw some fast bowling that might well have embarrassed any batting side in the world. At 151 Constantine, whose name can never be kept out of the score card for long, deceived Sutcliffe with a slower ball and bowled him, and at 159 Robinson touched a ball from Francis and was caught in the gully by the inevitable Constantine. Constantine followed this up by taking two wickets in two balls, bowling V.W.C. Jupp with a ball that the batsman made no attempt to play, but which came straight through to hit the middle stump, and getting Tate, who played a very indeterminate stroke, l-b-w. Unfortunately for Constantine's hopes of a hat trick J.W.H.T. Douglas was the next man in. Mr. Leveson-Gower's XI, however, had some very anxious moments before the follow-on was saved and, had E.L.G. Hoad at second slip held a catch Nunes offered him it was probable that Nunes could, if he wished, have sent them in again. Douglas, who later on was very unintelligently barracked by a portion of the crowd, had a thoroughly uncomfortable over from Francis, but he survived it and stayed not only to save the follow-on, but to hit two consecutive 4's off Griffith. At 206 Haig, hitting at Constantine who had the new ball, was beautifully caught by C.A. Roach at cover-point. A last wicket stand between Douglas and F.W. Gilligan materially decreased the West Indies' lead and it was not until 236 that Gilligan was caught in the slips off a ball of Constantine's that jumped.

–The Times,
Tuesday, September 11, 1928, Page 6

CONSTANTINE SIGNS FOR NELSON

L.N. Constantine, the West Indies all-round cricketer, yesterday signed an agreement for a three years' engagement with the Nelson Cricket Club. One of the clauses of the agreement stipulates that in the event of the West Indies team visiting England in the future, Constantine shall be allowed to play for them in Test Matches if his services are required, while another states that he will return to the West Indies at the close of each season.

–The Times,
Friday, September 21, 1928, Page 6

Select Bibliography

Books

A. Aspinall. - *The British West Indies: Their History, Resources and Progress* (London: Pitman, 1912)
A. Grimshaw (ed.). - *C.L.R. James: Cricket* (London: Allison and Busby, 1986)
B. Dobbs. - *The Edwardians at Play, Sport, 1890-1914* (London: Pelham, 1973)
B. Frindall. - *The Wisden Book of Test Cricket, 1876-1978* (London: Book Club, 1979)
B. Hamilton. - *Cricket in Barbados* (Bridgetown, Advocate, 1947)
B. Lawrence. - *100 Great West Indian Test Cricketers: From Challenor to Richards* (London: Hansib, 1988)
B. Lawrence. - *Master Class: The Biography of George Headley* (Leicester: Polar Press, 1995)
Barbados Cricket Association: *100 Years of Organized Cricket in Barbados* (Bridgetown: BCA, 1992)
C. Cummings. - "The Ideology of West Indian Cricket", Arena Review, 14, No. 1, 1990
C. Goodwin. - *Caribbean Cricketers from Pioneers to Packer* (London: Harrap, 1980)
C. Nicole. - *West Indian Cricket: The Story of Cricket in the West Indies* (London: Sportsman Book Club, 1960)
C.L.R. James. - *Beyond a Boundary* (London: Hutchinson, 1963)
C.L.R. James. - *Cricket* (London: Allison and Busby, 1989)
C.L.R. James. - *The Case for West Indian Self-Government* (London: Hogarth, 1933)
E.W. Swanton and G. Plumtree (eds.). - *Barclays World of Cricket: The Game from A-Z* (London: Willow Books, 1986)
F. Birbalsingh. - *The Rise of West Indies Cricket: From Colony to Nation* (London: Hansib, 1996)
G. Ross. - *A History of West Indies Cricket* (London: A. Barker, 1976)
G. Wolstenholme. - *The West Indies Tour to England, 1906* (Blackpool: Nelson, 1992)
G.J. Chester. - *Transatlantic Sketches, 1869* (Barbados: NCF, 1990)
H. Beckles with B. Stoddart (eds.). - *Liberation Cricket: West Indies Cricket Culture* (London: Manchester University Press, 1995)
H. Beckles. - *The Development of West Indies Cricket*, 2 vols. (London: Pluto Books; Kingston: University of the West Indies, 1999)
H.S. Altham and E.W. Swanton. - *A History of Cricket* (London: Allen and Unwin, 1948)
J. Grant. - *Jack Grant's Story* (London: Butterworths, 1980)
K. Sandiford. - *Cricket and the Victorians* (London: Solar Press, 1994)
L. Constantine. - *Cricket in the Sun* (London: Allan, 1947)
L. Constantine. - *Cricket and I* (London: Allan, 1933)
M. Manley. - *A History of West Indies Cricket* (London: André Deutsch, 1988)
P. Warner. - *Cricket between the Wars* (London: Chatto and Windus, 1942)
P. Warner. - *Lords, 1787-1945* (London: Harrap, 1946)
T. Cozier. - *The West Indies: Fifty Years of Test Cricket* (Newton Abbot: Devon Readers Union, 1978)

Bibliography

Newspapers and Magazines

Advocate News (Barbados)

Caribbean Cricket Quarterly

Chronicle (Guyana)

The Sporting Chronicle (England)

The Times (England)

Wisden Cricketers' Almanack

Wisden Cricket Monthly

Index

A NATION IMAGINED

78th Regiment 1
A. Priestly 8
A. Sandham 36
A.E. Harragin 14
A.E. Morton 17
A.P. Freeman 40, 42, 43, 52-54, 56, 59
A.P.F. Chapman 35, 40, 44, 51, 58
A.W. Carr 44
Berkenstad Club 35
Brian Stoddart 1
C. Hallows 40, 41, 43, 54
C. Roach 31, 45, 51, 54, 56, 58, 60, 61
C. Shankland 32
C.A. Ollivierre 11, 14, 19
C.L.R. James 1
C.P. Cumberbatch 9, 19
C.R. Browne 22, 25, 31, 45, 48, 52, 55, 57-60
C.V. Wight 25, 30, 31, 45, 51
Cambridge University 37
Carrington Club 11
Charles Lawrence 20
Clayton Goodwin 28
Clifford Goodman 19
Cox 14
Crystal Palace 13, 16
D.R. Jardine 40, 56
Derbyshire 15, 35
Donald Bradman 28
Dr. Gilbert Elliot 9
Dulwich 35
Durham/Northumberland 15
E. Tyldesley 40, 41, 51, 57, 59
E.A. McDonald 42
E.A. Rae 30-32, 45, 51, 61
E.L. Bartlett 30, 31, 45, 54, 58
E.L. Challenor 18
E.L.G. Hoad 30, 31, 45, 51, 54, 55, 58, 59, 61
Edgbaston 41
England XI 15
Essex 15, 24, 36, 60
F.R. Martin 31, 45, 50, 52, 53, 55, 59-61
Fenwicks 11
Fitz Hinds 11
Frank Birbalsingh 1
Frank Worrell 21
George Challenor 18, 21-25, 27, 28, 31, 37, 45, 52-54, 56, 58, 60, 61
G. Duckworth 58
G. Francis 22, 23, 27, 28, 31-33, 35-37, 45-47, 57, 60
G.A. Dewhurst 22, 50
G.C. Learmond 15
Garrison XI 1
Garrison 1
George Headley 49, 61-63
George John 22, 23, 28
George Wyatt 4, 7
Gerry Wolstenholme 15
Glamorgan 24, 57, 60
Gloucestershire 24, 42, 57, 60
H. Elliott 54, 58
H. Larwood 40, 42, 43, 52-54, 58
H. Smith 40, 54
H. Sutcliffe 35, 40, 41, 44, 52, 56, 57, 59
H.A. Cole 14
H.A. Cuke 29
H.B.G. Austin 22, 25, 27, 29, 32, 46, 47
H.D. Sewell 17
H.D.G. Leveson-Gower's XI 35, 59
H.G. Griffith 22, 31, 32, 35, 36, 45-47, 51, 57, 59-61
H.W. Ince 22
Hampshire 15, 59, 60
Harlequins 59, 60
Harrison College 25
Imperial Restaurant 16
Ireland XI 37, 60
J. Neblett 31, 45, 51
J. Woods 9, 11, 12, 14, 19
J.A. Small 21, 22, 30, 32, 45, 46, 48, 50, 52, 58, 60
J.C. White 54, 58

73

Index

J.E. Scheult 32
J.G. Kelshall 32
J.K. Holt 22
Jack Hobbs 35, 36, 40, 41, 43, 44, 54, 57, 59
Jeremiah Coleman 17
Jessop 14
Keith Sandiford 1
Kensington Oval 29, 42, 57
Kent XI 17
Kent 15, 59, 60
Krom Hendriks 21
L.K. Fyfe 7
L.N. Constantine 22, 23, 28, 31-33, 35-38, 45-47, 51-54, 57, 58, 60, 61
L.S. Constantine 11, 22
L.T. Yearwood 29, 32
Lancashire 42, 50
Leicestershire 15, 50, 57, 60
Llandudno 57
Lord Brackley 14
Lord Brackley's XI 15, 16
Lord Hawke 8, 9, 11, 20
Lord Tennyson 28, 31, 49
Lord Tennyson's XI 63
Lord's 17, 18, 29, 40, 41
M. Leyland 40, 58, 59
M.P. Fernandes 31, 45, 50, 60
M.W. Tate 40, 42, 43, 56, 59
Major G.S. Cox 32
MCC 15
MCC 7, 15, 17, 18, 25, 26, 28, 31, 37, 39, 42, 47, 50, 51, 60
Middlesex 28, 37, 38, 60
Minor Counties 15, 38, 60
Nelson 61
Norfolk 15
Northamptonshire 15, 24, 54, 60
Northumberland 37
Nottinghamshire 15, 18, 42
O.C. Scott 32, 45, 48, 51, 55, 58
Old Trafford 42, 54
Oxford University 24, 37, 60
P.A. Goodman 14
Pelham "Plum" Warner 9-12, 14, 18-20, 26
Percy Tarilton 21, 25, 30, 51
Pickwick Club 47
Queen's Park Cricket Club 15, 51
R. Phillips 22
R.H. Mallett 31
R.K. Nunes 32, 45, 49, 50, 54, 55, 57, 60
R.S. Warner 11
Reigate Priory 35
Rev. Grenville John Chester 2
Scotland 15
Sir Cavendish Boyle 16
Sir Julian Cahn's XI 59
Slade Lucas 7
Sonny Ramadhin 49
South Wales 15
Spartan 10, 11
St. Ann's Cricket Club 1
Surrey 15, 27, 37, 49
Sussex 27, 28, 59, 60
Sydney Smith 18, 19
The Oval 58, 59
V. Pascall 22
V.W.C. Jupp 40, 42, 52, 53, 56, 58
Victor Trumper 28
W. R. Hammond 40, 41, 42, 52, 56, 58
W. St. Hill 25, 30, 31, 45, 50, 51, 55, 58, 60
W.G. Grace XI 15, 16
W.G. Grace 4, 17
W.J. Burton 11
W.L.A. Coleman 13
Wanderers Club 25
West Indian Club 16
West Indies Cricket Board of Control 29, 31, 49
Wiltshire 15
Worcestershire 24, 54, 60
Yorkshire 15, 60

Other books on cricket by Hilary McD Beckles:

Editor:

Liberation Cricket: West Indies Cricket Culture [Manchester University Press, 1995, with Brian Stoddard],

An Area of Conquest: Popular Democracy and West Indies cricket [IRP, 1994: essays in honour of Sir Gary Sobers],

A Spirit of Dominance: Cricket and Nationalism in the West Indies, [UWI Press, 1998: essays in honour of Sir Viv Richards].

Author:

The Development of West Indies Cricket; Vol. 1 The Age of Nationalism; and *Vol. 2. The Age of Globalization* [UWI Press/ Pluto Press, 1999]